Changing Focus

The Future for Women
in the Canadian
Film and Television
Industry

TORONTO WOMEN IN FILM AND TELEVISION

© 1991 Foundation for Toronto Women in Film & Video
Printed in Canada by University of Toronto Press
This book is printed on recycled paper.

ISBN 0-9695351-0-4

Canadian Cataloguing in Publication Data

Main entry under title:

Changing focus: the future for women in the Canadian film and
television industry

Includes bibliographic references and index.
ISBN 0-9695351-0-4

1. Women in the motion picture industry – Canada.
2. Women in television broadcasting – Canada.
3. Toronto Women in Film and Television (Organization).

PN1995.9.W6C43 1991   384'.8'082   C91-094501-2

The funding for this publication was provided by the following
and it was produced with the participation of: Canada Employment and Immigration Commission; Department of Communications; Institut québécois du cinéma; National Film Board of
Canada; Ontario Film Development Corporation; Ontario
Women's Directorate; Secretary of State, Women's Program;
and Telefilm Canada.

Also available in French

Copies of this publication can be ordered from:
Toronto Women in Film and Television
150 John St., Suite 219
Toronto, Ontario, Canada M5V 3C3

Contents

Contents

Foreword

Change is not a vision in the distance. Change is upon us. And just as it is clear that we are in the midst of social and economic transformation, it is equally evident that issues of gender with their demands for a redistribution of power are in the forefront. *Changing Focus* and the *Statistical Profile of Women in the Canadian Film and Television Industry* (1990), which preceded it, are part of the dynamics of this process. These two reports were published by Toronto Women in Film and Television, an industry organization which represents women who work in every area of film and television. The *Statistical Profile* was undertaken because it became clear that there were no usable statistical data which reflected the patterns of work for women in our industries. In addition, it became clear that, without such data, the organization's advocacy efforts would be severely limited.

Changing Focus was developed to interpret and enrich the statistical data in the following ways: to examine the context out of which the original statistics arose; to explore issues of Industrial Relations, such as wage parity and employment equity; and to refine the concept of Voice and the right to expression which is at its heart. As well, a series of recommendations has been drawn together from the essays and are included in this document with the optimistic anticipation that they will form the basis for new initiative and policies.

For the most part in these essays, Industrial Relations topics encompass workplace specifics – employment equity, wage parity, problems of sexual harassment, child care, and career rhythm. These issues have been at the forefront of feminist thinking and advocacy for 20 years. If it seems all too familiar, the problem is not because the issues have become outdated. It is because discriminatory practices persist.

And although there are many variations of approach in these essays, one thing is clear. In the area of Industrial Relations, recommendations tend to demand that women share equally with men; that they have the same work opportunities; that they be represented in equal numbers in the workforce; and that they have the same pay scale. In other words, the demand is for a redistribution and re-allocation of the tangible and intangible resources in the industry.

Issues of Voice, the difficulties of public creative expression for those whose lives and persons do not conform to the institutionalized structures of power within our society, run like a subterranean river beneath the industrial relations material. And since issues of voice do not yield easily to dollar and hard number quantification, it is exceedingly difficult to highlight them when recommendations are being structured. Furthermore, unlike industrial relations, recommendations which rest on the more comfortable ideal of gender equality, issues of Voice lead to one of the most contentious items on the political agenda today – Entitlement to Difference. And, to truly address Entitlement to Difference in the context of our industry, would require the redefinition of all existing notions of power. As a result, it is fair to say that future breakthroughs in industrial relations may well depend on changes of policy; but breakthroughs in the area of Voice will depend on changes of heart.

Moreover, clarification within the debate on Voice can only occur if the participants are prepared to address the fact that systemic discrimination is rife in our industry; that women who attempt to explore and articulate it are rendered powerless; and that the debate is impossible when the opposition appears incapable of acknowledging that the issue exists.

Changing Focus makes clear that the structures of the film and television industry in both the public and private sectors harbour particularly pernicious forms of systemic discrimination. For example, "Gatekeepers," those with the power to say "yes" or "no" to a project, are found everywhere in the industry, and they do not seem to grasp that their selection criteria demand that women perform as men. They convert discussions of Voice into discussions of Industrial Relations; and they impose terms of equality where *only* terms of difference are appropriate. They believe that they are applying objective standards based on notions of quality, when, in fact, they are applying historically conditioned, subjective terms of reference established by men. And these Gatekeepers are convinced of their own neutrality. They have failed to understand that neither they, nor the products of the industry in which they work, can ever be politically neutral. Their passivity masks their vested interest in preserving a faltering and non-adaptive status quo and results in products that are powerfully regressive.

The contributors to *Changing Focus* are determined to move the Industrial Relations agenda forward. But they are also declaring that it is not the only agenda. In broadening the dialogue to include Voice, they are bringing forward the vexing and complex ideas that surround it.

It is essential that all of us begin to question the axioms which have shaped our work and our world. It is not enough for women to be given equal opportunity and equal money to make programs and products like men; they must also find the power to alter the nature and the essence of the products they make. And these goals must be achieved not just because it is the way for more women to take their rightful place at the core of our industry, but because the products created by our industry shape the identities, the myths, and the values of our society.

It is common practice to observe that when the Voice of women is denied access through the system, the experience of 52 per cent of the nation's population is denied. In fact, given the power of mass communications, this denial does not affect 52 per cent of the population, it affects 100 per cent. Every one of us, male and female alike.

It is not just time to renegotiate the Industrial Contract, which has been so limiting for the women who work in the film and television industries, we must renegotiate as well the Social Contract, which has kept their Voices to a whisper.

Annette Cohen
Producer

Preface

In 1985, members of Toronto Women in Film and Television (formerly Toronto Women in Film and Video) gave the organization a mandate to try to improve opportunities for women in the film and television industry. At that time, there was plenty of anecdotal evidence that women's participation in the industry was low, particularly in the high-status, high-income positions, but there was little concrete data available. Nevertheless, key industry leaders seemed to be of the opinion that many women were successful in the film and television industry. By naming a small number of prominent women, these people felt they could demonstrate that women in fact "had arrived." Our desire for accurate statistical data sprang from that generally held impression – which we as women believed to be wrong. We were indeed positive that this was a myth but felt that only hard data would convince the sceptics and that the research should be undertaken by a totally disinterested group. In 1990, therefore, TWIFT commissioned a report from the independent consulting firm Peat Marwick Stevenson & Kellogg which was released in spring 1990 as *A Statistical Profile of Women in the Canadian Film and Television Industry*. That report gathered together 200 pages of statistics on the participation rate of women in every segment of the film and television industry without commentary or analysis.

The figures make very clear that, in this industry, women are participating at an outrageously low rate in each job category – apart from those jobs our organization refers to as "pink-collar ghettos": low-income, low-status support jobs.

The figures also suggest a profound social problem: while the film and television industry is an industry like any other, producing products for sale, it stands apart from others in that, in Canada, it provides one of our most important means of communicating with one another; excluding women from this communication process means that women, who are over 50 per cent of our population, are denied voice. As a silenced majority women cannot speak out about issues, share their concerns, or put forward their perspective. Dramas rarely present a female protagonist in stories written by women; current affairs coverage rarely includes women experts and still treats female political candidates in a different way from the way it treats men.

Furthermore, the film and television industry has a tremendous impact on our culture: it creates imagery that permeates our unconscious and provides role models for our young people. With this in mind, if we recognize a need to have women be full participants in the fabric of our society, we cannot afford to continue to exclude a female presence and perspective.

Early in 1991, a Toronto *Star* columnist listed the names of a few prominent media women and concluded that women were taking over the communications industry. The *Statistical Profile* provides concrete evidence that this is not the case. Despite the presence of many talented, prominent, and successful women, the overall situation for women is grim. The dismal fact is that we have made little progress ove the years, and we can only conclude that the process of evolutionary change has not and is not likely to help women gain entry to this industry. (Indeed the position of women in the industry in Canada is echoed in other parts of the world. In the United States, women are in a similar situation. The Director's Guild of America released statistics in 1991 reporting that of 7332 feature films made by its members between 1939 and 1979, only 14 were directed by women and those 14 were directed by seven women.)

Change can only take place if people want change. A conscious effort on the part of both men and women to choose another path is our only hope.

Now, a year after our first report, we are pleased to present *Changing Focus*, which analyses the data, comments on it, and, finally, makes recommendations which are, in essence, a plan of action. In this plan we assign work for everyone associated with this industry, both public and private sectors, as well as for our own organization. The result, we hope, will be that within a reasonable period of time equality for women working in the film and television industry will become a reality.

This report could not have been prepared without the contribution of many people, working as an energetic and enthusiastic team. The names of some are found elsewhere in this book, but there are others who contributed at earlier stages whose assistance was key. Although they cannot all be named here, we are conscious of what we owe them.

Our first thanks must go to our project funders who thought our efforts worth backing. Their names are found on page iv. Certain individuals were particularly helpful to us: Eric Ferguson and Nancy Green of the Canada Employment and Immigration Commission, Susan McMurray of the Ontario Women's Directorate, Robin Jackson and Guy Mayson of the Department of Communications, Bernard Boucher of the Institut québécois du cinéma, James Weyman of the Ontario Film Development Corporation, Helen Doyon of the Department of Secretary of State, and Michaelle McLean of Telefilm Canada. A special thanks goes to Suzanne Chevigny of the National Film Board of Canada who acted as our liaison with our Quebec counterpart organizations and with the Quebec authors. Without her help, this report could not have had its present scope.

Our next debt is to our writers who make a formidable team of experts. They bring a wide range of experience and perspectives from the worlds of academe, law, journalism, and the film and television industry to their analysis and commentary found in these pages.

The members of Toronto Women in Film and Television also deserve a very special thanks, in particular President Barbara Barde and, working closely with her, the members of the board, as well as Policy Committee members Annette Cohen, Karen Laurence, and Kay Armatage, and past-president Penny Hynam. Office manager Denise Mulvey has been helpful throughout, as has our publicist Joanne Smale. The film and television industry in general has supported the work. Members of the Canada Employment and Immigration Joint Adjustment Committee served as the steering committee for the project and gave their time, their ideas, and their contacts to help this project to completion. They are:

Chair Susan Douglas Rubes, producer/performer
Project Coordinator Elaine Waisglass, screenwriter/artist
Industry Representatives
Mary Ambrose, ACTRA

Susanne Chevigny, director, Employment Equity Program, National Film
    Board
Anna-Sue Greenberg, public affairs coordinator, Astral Bellevue Pathe
Don Haig, producer
Meg Hogarth, national president, ACTRA
Edward Trapunski, producer
Canada Employment and Immigration Representative
Nancy Green, industrial adjustment consultant
Ontario Women's Directorate Representative
Susan McMurray, employer liaison officer
Toronto Women in Film and Television Representatives
Barbara Barde, president
Penelope Hynam, past president
Jean McDougall, project treasurer
Elaine Waisglass, co-chair, Policy Committee

Finally, there are those who helped organize the funding, put this document together, and sent it out. Jean McDougall, project treasurer, has controlled the administrative aspects of our work including the challenge of trying to ensure that all elements of our budget and expenses came together at appropriate times. Mary McDougall Maude of Shipton, McDougall Maude Associates managed the editorial process from the planning stages, with key textual assistance from Rosemary Shipton. Susan Crean, Diane Silverman, and Albanie Morin undertook a series of interviews which were used by Pat Armstrong and Susan Crean in their articles. SIDAC Group Inc. provided translation and editing services under severe pressures of time. Jacqueline Généreux reviewed the French text. All those involved in the final assembly of the book worked under great pressure: Liz Driver who prepared the index, Gwen Peroni who supplied the pages, Will Rueter who designed the book, and Laurie Lewis of Campus Printing and Design who managed the printing. Our thanks go also to Joy Williams and Frances Gambino of Heather Reid and Associates who took charge of the release of *Changing Focus*.

Elaine Waisglass
Co-chair, Policy Committee
Coordinator, Statistical Profile Project

Introduction to the Essays

Changing Focus: The Future of Women in the Canadian Film and Television Industry examines the involvement of women in this industry. It began as a study of employment and access to it. The statistics collected by Peat Marwick Stevenson & Kellogg and presented in its report, *A Statistical Profile of Women in the Canadian Film and Television Industry* (1990), represent the raw numbers of how many people – men and women – are working in what jobs and sectors of the industry, in what provinces, and what they earn. Looking at the mainstream of the industry, it documents government investment through its funding agencies, as well as education and training, and awards.

These statistics reveal that although women now form over 44 per cent of the workforce in Canada, we are only 35 per cent of the workforce in the film and television industry. They reveal that women dominate in certain job categories. Of 51 categories in the private sector women hold between 70 and 93 per cent of the jobs in six categories: production secretary/bookkeeper, script supervisor/continuity, art department trainee, wardrobe, makeup artist, hairstylist. In 1989 women held 14 per cent of the upper management jobs in public sector television/radio companies; in the private sector they held 1 per cent. Salaries were consistently lower for women than for the men in the private sector, and even in the public sector average salaries for men were higher. The figures on investment revealed that most of the funds allocated for production went to projects produced, directed, and written by men in all areas; for example, Telefilm Canada figures reveal that, in 1987-88, women producers received only 9 per cent of funds.

The figures depict what the situation was at a given point in time in great detail. By themselves, however, they are meaningless to most people. They do not indicate why the situation they describe exists or how it might be changed. The articles in *Changing Focus* consist of an analysis of the statistics and an examination of why the current situation exists.

Pat Armstrong's article provides an in-depth look at the statistics for the industry, and she uses a series of interviews with women in the industry (done for this study) to give concrete examples of what the numbers mean. Margaret Visser and Susan Crean look at different aspects of the attitudes, assumptions, and prejudices prevalent in our society that lie behind what the figures reveal. The articles by Linda Silver Dranoff and Kealy Wilkinson examine the legal and policy underpinnings of the current state of women in the industry. Linda Lewis, in her article, looks at the education of women in the industry, and her report on educational institutions casts doubt on the ability of post-secondary institutions in general to educate women. Several writers, Louise Surprenant, Iolande Cadrin-Rossignol and Louise Lamarre, and Armande Saint-Jean, look at the situation in Quebec, which has developed somewhat differently from English Canada for historic and cultural reasons. Jocelyne Denault and Kay Armatage provide some historic background to the situation women find themselves in today, and it is refreshing to read the two perspectives on the National Film Board in Canada, one looking from English Canada and one from Quebec, between two covers. These articles all look at women in general, but of course women encompass many, many groups, all with different interests, expectations, and viewpoints. Rita Shelton Deverell, Lisa Airst, and Daisy Lee discuss what it is like for the other "designated groups" – visible minorities, aboriginal peoples, people with disabilities – to work, or try to work, in this industry. Paula Caplan examines from a psychological point of view the concept of merit and how it applies to decisions in our society: what lies behind which script gets funded or which picture gets made.

Certain themes emerge strongly from these articles, but the overwhelming message is a simple one. The institutions of our society were developed by and for men. They reflect the working and living patterns and values of men. Women are not welcomed in the upper echelons of the structures. Women are not always welcomed in the lower echelons of the structures in areas that have traditionally been occupied by men. Our styles of working are different from those of men, our ways of communication are different, our family and home responsibilities remain stubbornly different. We are not comfortable within male structures, and men are not comfortable having us there.

Recognizing the problem is but one step towards a solution. In fact, of course, the problem was recognized long ago. Effecting the kind of change that is necessary to ensure full partnership for women is extremely difficult. Part three of *Changing Focus* looks at what might be done within the film and television industry to ensure equality for women. These recommendations for change grew out of the articles and the writers' suggestions. They were reviewed at length by our Joint Adjustment Committee. Various government agencies and departments were asked to comment on them in an informal way, and several groups from the industry as a whole were asked to make suggestions and comments. Our plan of action then has grown out of a fairly long consultative process with women and men in the industry and in government. We hope the recommendations will form the basis for substantial change.

The need for this change cannot be overemphasized. *Changing Focus* grew out of what was primarily a study of employment. Underlying that, however, is the link between employment and what we see on our screens. This link is recognized in the new Broadcasting Act. How do we ensure that all aspects of life and culture in Canada are reflected in what is portrayed in films and on television? How do we pass on to our children our values and teach them the things we think important? One way – and it is perhaps the least intrusive way – is to ensure that all segments of our society are able to put forward their points of view. Women's points of view are at present represented in only a marginal way. Women form over 50 per cent of the population of the country. It is past time for our perspective to have equal billing.

Part One   WHAT DO THE NUMBERS MEAN?

PAT ARMSTRONG

1 Understanding the Numbers: Women in the Canadian film and television industry

There's no business like show business, the old song says. There are, of course, many similarities with other industries. Especially in the public sector, the entertainment business has increasingly developed a corporate structure little different from the rest. Like other businesses, the entertainment business has secretaries and senior executives; nine-to-five workers and pension plans. And habits, attitudes, and practices shared with other businesses are reflected in the continuing segregation of women into the least prestigious jobs at wages significantly lower than that of men.

But show business also has its own particular characteristics, its own particular habits, attitudes, and practices. Patterns of segregation, harassment, and exclusion found elsewhere are frequently exaggerated in this business. When the focus is on mainstream television and film, as is the case here, it becomes evident that the women in show business often have a tougher time than the men.

THE ENTERTAINMENT BUSINESS

According to a producer and production manager in a private film company, when you want to find out about women's place in this industry "you have to look at how business works as a business because the entertainment business – show business – is just that; it is a business like anything else."[1] He went on to say that he "thinks women can do anything they want. It is just [a question of] how good they are." However, he also pointed out that

very rarely [is] a woman gonna be grips or electrics or those traditional areas that require physical strength. But then again almost every script supervisor I've ever met is female, because it is more of a detail bookish discipline ... I found that the majority of the people that I've worked with are quite respectful of the women that they are working with in the industry and judge them no more harshly than they do men, just so much as they hold up their end. I think that you will find that there is little time or respect for frailty and traditionally females have been more frail than males in society and frankly there is not time for that in the film industry.

Another male involved in production work also emphasized that television and film are businesses like the rest. In his view as well there are no particular constraints on women in this industry.

I don't think there are any barriers outside, I think there are barriers inside. Women's own attitudes which have been formed by a male-dominated world ... If you want to be in any business, you better find out what that business is all about including prejudice and all the rest of it, just as a man must ... I think one of the dangers in the women's movement today tends to be that it becomes the cop-out reason, the reason for not making it because I am a woman. Now, there is no question; a woman may have more difficulty because of habits that have been ingrained and all the rest of it over time. I don't have to go over this. There are habits and things that go down. But if you're tough and you're strong, you can win ... But there are no habits in the film industry ... There are habits in our modern society that men are macho and women are feminine, and those habits are being, trying to be, changed around for good reason. So it is hard ... for some men to accept women as equal and it is hard for some women to take the leadership role ... So that's got to be understood if women are to make the stride, so they're gonna have as much guts and perseverance and understanding; that is the nature of the beast ... just somehow the chutzpah, balls and the guts to do it, but it is not a female thing in my view.

A woman producer agreed that the structure of the film and television industry is similar in many ways to other business organizations, although her perspective was somewhat different.

There's all the traditional things I think you would find operating in any male-controlled environment. By controlled, I mean male-shaped. I mean it isn't just that the gatekeeper is male, it's the tradition of the male organizational structure. I could call it patriarchal structure, but I'm talking more pragmatically than that.

She too blamed part of the problem on culture. "Our culture has trained women to back away from power." But, she added, "I don't want women to blame themselves. Nothing outrages me more ... Not that I get mad at the women, but so angry that women blame themselves in that classic victim way. For what? Nothing. They are culturally ground down."

The data collected for Toronto Women in Film and Video support at least part of the claim that women here face many of the same constraints and opportunities as women in other areas.

"HABITS IN MODERN SOCIETY": PARALLELS WITH EMPLOYMENT IN OTHER INDUSTRIES

Some Signs of Progress: The Visible Women
Like women in other industries, women in the film and television business have made some progress in recent years. At least one woman has moved into almost every occupation previously dominated by men, including some of the most senior positions. Another male producer explained:

There are more women who are writing and getting their work produced and there are more women who are directing and getting their work produced, there are more women in the technical side of the business, but, whether or not this is a significant increase over 15 years, the truth is I cannot tell you ...

It is difficult to find statistics that would make it possible to examine the changes in women's film and television work over time. But according to the Toronto Women and Film data, women are now represented in all but two job categories.

Women seem to be everywhere in film and television today. Patricia Rozema's *White Room* introduced a 1990 film retrospective in Paris organized by Toronto's Festival of Festivals and the Cinémathèque Ontario. Mireille Dansereau won "le premier prix comme réalisatrice" in "une grande competition dans tous les pays du Commonwealth" a number of years ago. The head of CBC's Newsworld is a woman and so is its director of television news and current affairs. There are women reading the news, women listed in the credits as grips, sound editors, camera operators, and mixers. But the visibility of these high-profile women camouflages the fact that women are scarce at the top and plentiful at the bottom of the film and television industry.

Continuing Segregation Behind the Scenes
Like women in other industries, most women in television and film remain segregated into women's jobs in the least powerful positions of the occupational hierarchy. Their precise location varies with region, with the nature of the production, with the sector, and with the content. This is perhaps why a senior male in the public television sector could say of the figures cited in the 1990 study *A Statistical Profile of Women in the Canadian Film and Television Industry*:

when you walk around and look at what the statistics say, there seems to be some sort of ... either something new has happened since the statistics were compiled, which I suspect is the case, or the statistics somehow missed the whole picture. But just within

... creative management ... the area heads and senior line management which would be the people running the different divisions administratively – of the creative management, the majority are women, the line management 50-50, the executive producers – it is a huge majority of women.

He went on to note, however, that "you are probably right on sports and news ... [they're] traditionally male-dominated in rank and file, particularly on the technical side." And in financing,

there still is, I think, in parts of broadcasting an old boys' club and I think that it is tough to break when you are outside that circle. Whether you are outside of that circle because you are a woman or because you are an ethnic or because you are a visible minority or because you didn't go to the right school ... I think there is a varying level of discrimination.

From the perspective of a senior manager within certain areas of the CBC, it may seem like women have taken over, but sober second thought – and the data – indicate that this is far from the case. Women are underrepresented at the senior management and creative levels, both in relation to males and in relation to women's overall share of the jobs in the media, even within most areas of the CBC and the National Film Board.

In the Public Sector
There are more women working in the public sector and more women in senior management and creative positions in the public sector than there are in the private sector. Women account for 37 per cent of those working in the public sector of the industry, compared to 34 per cent of the private sector.[2] Women's overall share of broadcast work in the public and private sectors is relatively equal but women in the public sector make up a much larger proportion (52 per cent) of those working in production than they do in the private sector (27 per cent). With 65 per cent of the distribution work and only 27 per cent of the production work, women in the private sector are disproportionately segregated into the least creative areas of employment.

Public Sector Film Production – National Film Board
Compared to other sectors of the industry, women have their best chance in the public film corporation. At the National Film Board, women account for almost a third of the senior and middle managers, more than a third of the filmmakers, over half of the scientific and professional staff. This is less than their 44 per cent share of the entire labour force but better than their share of private industry. Indeed, more than half of those working at the NFB are women.

But these numbers hide some very real segregation within the Film Board. Most obviously, women's share of senior managerial and creative jobs is significantly less than their share of all jobs in the sector. Less obviously, women at the top are less likely than men to have secure employment. One of the four women in senior management has a term job and she is the only senior manager without a continuous contract. Three-quarters of the scientific and professional staff without secure jobs are women. Similarly, all of the producers and nearly two-thirds of the directors on term contracts are women.[3]

Of the appointments made in 1987-88, 32 went to women but 27 of the new jobs were in term positions. And although women represent close to half of the distribution and information staff, the number of women in continuing jobs decreased by 14 per cent between 1987 and 1989. Women's increased participation in this area was entirely in term positions. Those women in these term jobs could be out of work today and many would certainly be the first to find themselves without work if there are more cutbacks. Women are the most flexible part of the NFB labour force and therefore will bear the brunt of current austerity schemes. Indeed, reductions in federal funding could mean that women no longer have their best chance in the public film corporation.

Moreover, women producers and directors are segregated within the NFB into the least prestigious areas. As a study of the film board has shown: "Female producers are to be found, although unevenly, in animation, documentary and multi-media films, for the most part."[4] Multi-media, where women are most successful in their direct competition with men, is, as one producer explained, "sort of the bottom level because they make the slide shows and the film strips." Men, on the other hand, were found in all areas and they dominate fiction production, the most recognized and expensive productions. Although two-thirds of the English multi-media productions were directed by women, this was the case for only a quarter of the fiction films.[5]

Women producers and directors were also disproportionately located within Studio D and the Federal Women's Film Program doing "women's films." In fact, if the special women's studios were closed at NFB, over half the female producers and directors would disappear but almost all the men would stay. These studios provide opportunities for women who would not otherwise be able to make films, especially with this content, and demonstrate the importance of introducing special programs for women. However, they can also serve to justify women's limited access to other areas and to working with other kinds of content. A woman filmmaker sees Studio D as "very supportive of a very select crowd ... It's all right for some women" but entry into others studios she found more difficult.

I mean, I'd go to the big cheese of the film board and sit down and ask for something and I'd walk out of there crying because I'd been so intimidated ... on the other hand, by most of my peers I'm considered tough. Yet I'd walk into the office of the big cheese and just be completely intimidated. I think not because I'm so easily intimidated but because they're such prigs.

There are other aspects of segregation hidden by the overall numbers as well. For example, the number of women listed in these job categories does not necessarily indicate how many films they produce or control. In 1985-86, women accounted for a third of the producers but for less than a quarter of the films produced. And while it was common to find men in all areas both producing and directing films, it was "quite exceptional to find films both produced and directed by women" and these exceptions were found mainly in multimedia and documentaries.[6] They were also found mainly in the special women's studios. Women producers and directors have been receiving an increasing share of the NFB budget, but here too their share is greatest in short films and multi-media, not feature or animation films.

The focus on the most visible jobs also draws attention away from the extensive segregation in other areas of the NFB. Most of the men who are employed at NFB are directly involved in making films; most of the women are not. Over half of the women working there are part of the office staff; only 5 per cent of the men are office staff. Women also make up two-thirds of the administrative staff. At the same time, few women do technical or cinematography work. Only 17 per cent of the continuing technicians are women while they account for more than two-thirds of those employed on term contracts in these jobs. Meanwhile 93 per cent of the cinematographers are men.

Women have made progress within the film board. A great deal of this progress reflects the introduction of programs designed to encourage the hiring, funding, training, and promotion of women. A woman who now makes films complained that she is

very resentful that Studio D never supported me as a sound technician ... As a sound technician I went to Studio D every day practically, until I was convinced I was a regular pain in the ass and yet they never recognized that I took a course, even though I was recording sound in private industry.

She went on to explain, however, that today

the film board has a very good equity program which involves the money, a fund of money ... for the engagement of women on crews ... if I choose to make a film in which I want a woman on the crew and there's not a woman on staff available – which of course there's not – they will make the money available. That's even better than hiring one woman. It's infinitely more interesting than hiring one camera woman, one sound woman, because she may or may not be good and ... there would be tremendous pressure on her to be great. But if you have a fund that allows, when you think you'd like to work with a woman technician, to hire her, it's not as expensive as putting a woman on staff ... It gives a whole lot of women the experience. It's a real incentive to hire women ...

Such programs have resulted in real gains for women, and the figures given in the *Statistical Profile* reflect that change. But the high proportion of women working on term contracts indicates that these gains may only be temporary. And the concentration of filmmakers in the women's studios and in particular kinds of productions suggests the precarious nature of these gains. The continuing male domination of all but the administrative and professional work demonstrates that women still have a long way to go before they are equitably and permanently represented throughout the NFB.

Public Sector Broadcasting – CBC

Like the Film Board, the CBC has a better record than the private sector. According to data collected under employment equity legislation, women in public sector radio and television have a greater share of all jobs and a greater share of managerial, technical, and professional work than women in private radio and television. Moreover, women's position as non-contract producers and executive producers has improved relative to that of men, although this has been primarily a result of the decline in males in non-contract positions rather than increases in the number of women hired for non-contract producer jobs.

According to employment equity data, women in public radio and television hold 14 per cent of upper level management positions, compared to 7 per cent in the private sector. In the words of a woman senior manager, ''the CBC has an environment that promotes women ... We're beyond hiring women as tokens. We're now hiring women who have the credibility, who have the talent and the strengths and can move into those positions.'' Another maintained:

it has happened basically because there were two factors. First of all, a large number of women were brought in at lower levels, so there is now a pool of qualified women – and this is especially true now – a pool of qualified women for all jobs. Secondly, the corporation itself undertook programs of affirmative action and that made sure that the women who were there and were talented were promoted.

But these signs of progress should not detract attention from the very high levels of segregation that remain. According to CBC figures on regular employees (as opposed to contract), there are no women senior producers or

NABET camera operators and there is only one woman in technical production and in maintenance work. As a senior manager pointed out, "we don't have a lot of women cameramen, we don't have a lot of women sound men or lighting." Although women make up more than a third of the total CBC radio and television workforce, they account for less than 15 per cent of the middle managers and executive producers and only a quarter of senior managers, producers, set designers, and film editors. Meanwhile, they are more than two-thirds of the costume makers, make-up artists, and production or script assistants, the traditional female jobs near the bottom of the hierarchy.

Although the female participation rate is quite consistent across provinces, the segregation is not. Women account for three out of the four directors in Prince Edward Island but less than a third of the directors in Quebec and only one in ten of those in Alberta. These considerable variations offer some indication of why the producer quoted earlier claimed the statistics are wrong at the same time as they suggest that even women's current position is far from secure.

Not only do women remain segregated into female-dominated jobs and excluded from some male-dominated ones. Those who do make it into traditional male areas seldom have an easy time. "I think most women have a tough time when their first jobs as manager comes up, and yeah, there is that resistance," said a senior woman at the CBC.

I mean one of the guys who promoted me, encouraged me, was my friend, said to me once, "You know, I just do not feel comfortable when you're in a meeting: I don't feel comfortable working with a woman." And this was a guy, as I said, who had stepped out of those feelings ... had given me jobs, had encouraged me, had always treated me equally and fairly, and yet he told me he had these feelings of discomfort. Now if he has those feelings, you can imagine what the general run of men have.

In spite of improvements, the culture is male and women have to battle constantly to prevent exclusion. The same women who praised the environment at CBC went on to say that

sexist is probably as good a descriptive as anything. There are men, and I would tend to say the men from the old boys' network, who look on a younger woman who's getting ahead or just looking on a woman. I know there are many producers that came in the door to pitch me ideas, and they felt insecure. I guess that's the best way of describing it. The gentlest way of characterizing it. They feel insecure in the presence of a woman. They feel insecure in the presence of a woman and particularly of a woman that has power ... They call you dear, they're patronizing ... You'd extend your hand and someone wouldn't shake hands ... We're always dealing with the sexist comments.

But, as a senior woman on the creative side explained, these kinds of attitudes are not restricted to older men. "I think that some of them have trouble when it comes down to the crunch, have trouble accepting a woman as a creative equal on set. That's all I can think it is. It is interesting because the ones that I've had this problem with are the ones my age. I am 37."

Difficult as things may be inside the CBC, senior women have even more problems when they go outside the corporation. A manager since she turned 33, the other woman quoted above talked about her membership on a board she participates in by virtue of her position at CBC.

I am the only woman that has ever been on the board and its a long time since I've had that feeling of being an object of real curiosity and some – not exactly hostility – but suspicion. I walk into that room and the smell of testosterone almost knocks you over.

This same woman went on to caution that the progress at CBC has been largely limited to women in positions near the top.

I'm really talking about the experience [of] professional women and executive women, and I think there is a wide gap between their experience and the experience of people at the lower levels. I think that things have changed radically for women who are professionals and who are managers, but I don't think they've changed that much for women who are clerical or who are support staff or who hope to have technical jobs. To me, life really goes on in very traditional ways at that level.

A female sound technician explained, "it's real male dominated and continues to be ... People don't think women can hold a tape recorder or understand the camera or lift a light." Another woman sound recordist is convinced that if she had been a male, she would have

made more money and would have gotten more work, just because there aren't any women out there doing it. I never met another woman recordist. I never met another woman who does boom ... I have worked with a woman grip once and I think that is the extent of the women I have worked with over the years as technician ... I would say 99.9 per cent of the people doing the hiring have never heard of women doing that position, then why would they have any great faith that that person could carry it off?

Her suppositions were confirmed by a male private sector producer who explained: "you can't be a grip, you can't be in electric, you can't be a generator operator, because those are traditionally very physically demanding male jobs although I do know a couple of female grips [who] are tough." These women not only face opposition and attitudes about appropriate women's work; they also face them alone.

Like women in management, women technicians must operate in a male culture.

There is something that happens when you walk onto a set or onto a stage when you're setting up technical equipment and you are the only woman in the room. I think that that feels a little uncomfortable for the people around you because they're used to relating to each other in a certain way and once you introduce that new element, that creates a little discomfort because they feel unsure about their footing as to whether they can continue to interact in the same way that they have built up over the years as almost [a] boys' club.

According to a woman in the electric and grip department,

In the technical group, the males are very male to a certain degree and they are not the nice guys on the set and they are not the businessmen on the set and that is one of the strongest things that I say for a female is being able to put up with that.

A woman sound editor ''was in a field that was a sort of non-traditional kind of job and I was always kind of proud about that but it was also lonely because there were not that many women.''

The problems female technicians face, this same sound recordist explained, reflect both past and current practices.

Historically, they haven't been exposed to or trained in technical areas and the level of self-confidence in technical areas that women have is very, very low and also the expectations that men have for women to know about these things is very low and the combination of those two things has played a rather disastrous role in women in this industry.

A woman sound editor who did not really see any barriers to women in the field still talked about remarks like: '' 'Don't move that heavy machine when you're a woman,' that kind of thing. I know a number of men sort of say that, or, 'She won't know about that technical thing, she's a woman.' ''

These attitudes and practices not only serve to exclude women from some jobs but they also serve to favour them in others. A woman who now works as a sound editor was told:

It's nice to have a woman around because they are pretty to look at ... it was nice to have a woman assistant or women should be assistants. I think that men were open to women being assistant whereas they may not have been as open to hiring a man as an assistant and/or [may think] that women were more organized, which is basically what the assistants job required ... Some people think that, you know,'cause women are nicer, more pleasant or maybe more docile ... it is easier to have a woman assistant than a male assistant.

In the words of an assistant director, "they look at it as easier for you to be an underling."

It's also easier in office work. A woman producer, who found it "very tough" to break into film, "was pretty quickly shown that I would be accepted in administrative positions even if they involve creative, but not in technical or directing." "The CBC in particular suggested that I spend a year or two, probably working as a clerk," reported a woman who now does continuity.

Such clerical jobs can provide a way in for women, up a route than seems to be particularly female. This was the path for a woman who currently works as a first assistant director.

In order to get into production at CBC at that time and also at this time, you still have to get on staff somehow. I had managed to get my typing skills up to a sufficient level to get hired as a production secretary. In the variety department. But almost immediately after I got on the staff at CBC, there was an opening for a script assistant and I was interviewed and met the requirements that they had at that time. And I was then trained as a script assistant for various shows in the children's department.

As a woman casting director explained: "Most of the women I know got a foot in the door by, god knows, typing scripts somewhere or answering phones somewhere. And, sure, the men didn't have to do that, but that doesn't mean that the women couldn't go as far as the men in the long run."

But the run is much longer and more difficult for women. It is usually through the less prestigious areas, like children's programs, that have been associated with women's traditional skills. And, not surprisingly given the barriers women face, many drop out along the way or remain typing scripts. According to a woman producer,

a lot of them don't stay in the industry. A lot of them stay at the lowest level of the industry. A lot of them get brought in at the secretarial level and get fed up after a while and go somewhere else. Men are going to technical fields, and they sometimes start as assistant cameramen. They go into sound and hang in, from what I can see, for far longer, at far more productive levels, than the women do.

Starting in the typing jobs does more than discourage women from remaining in the industry. It also serves to reinforce the notions about women's skills and place.

These routes through traditional female jobs, combined with formalized hiring practice, affirmative action programs, and methods for monitoring progress, all help explain why women do better at the CBC and NFB than they do elsewhere. They demonstrate that concerted efforts can lead to real gains for women. But the continuing segregation in terms of content areas and in terms of jobs points to the problems with these old routes and to the need for programs directed not only at getting women in but at making sure that all aspects of the industry are open to them. And opening areas to them requires changing cultures as well as policies.

In the Private Sector

The segregation in the private sector is very similar to that in the public sector but it is more exaggerated in most areas. It varies by segment, by function, by production, and by company, but it never disappears.

Within the private sector, women are best represented in distribution, an area that is American-dominated. Women account for two-thirds of those working in this segment of private industry. Although this is not the most creative area in the industry, it is a powerful one because distribution involves, in the words of a major distributor, "working towards the acquisition of a film, whether it be the finished film or a film at the script stage."

Most of the women who work here, however, are not making decisions about which films we see. Forty per cent of them do clerical work and fewer than a third are at the senior management level. Fewer still make the final decisions. Although she knows "a lot of women in the distribution business," an independent distributor thought there were only "one or two" in Canada who own their own business. When she did work for others, she found she "was never quite trusted for financial acumen or business acumen or deal making at a certain level." She does, however, "think women make better sales persons because they listen differently. I think we have a different way of hearing and I think it makes you good at selling which is what I have to do." But selling jobs are not the most influential jobs in this segment of the industry.

Women's representation in the broadcast sector is significantly less than it is in distribution. Here, they account for only 37 per cent of the labour force although their share of jobs is virtually the same as women's share of jobs in public sector broadcasting. Within broadcasting, their share is greatest in cable television, where the least production and on-air work is done. Women have 43 per cent of the jobs in cable television, compared to less than a third in other private radio and television.

Within private broadcasting, women are more segregated than they are in the public sector. Women represent only 7 per cent of upper management, compared to 14 per cent in the public sector, and only 1 per cent in private radio and television. They do slightly better in middle or other management, especially in cable television. Many may well be permanently at these lower managerial levels, however. A senior woman manager in private television has seen, in both the private and public sectors, women who are "not able to bust through that glass ceiling into management and their career is stalling."

Women are better represented in the professional as opposed to the managerial category, especially in private television. Thirty-eight per cent of the professionals in private television are women. However, a third of them are either temporary or part-time. This is the case for only 15 per cent of the male professionals. In terms of daily practice, these professional women may fare no better than female managers. "I could mention hundreds of incidents" said a woman lawyer, "where clients and other people have reacted to me firstly in ... a male-female way and secondly as a lawyer-client or business relationship. You know, men ask me out to dinner and talk about my social schedule and where it is clearly inappropriate."

While the predominance of male clients affects women professionals, the predominance of male professionals affects clients. From this lawyer's perspective, "it is not uncommon for lawyers in particular to view their female clients with a little less respect [than] their male producer clients."

Most of the clients these professionals serve are men. The semi-professional and technical category – which in terms of the employment equity data used here includes directors and producers, performers, announcers, and equipment operators – is 80 per cent male in the full-time work. Women are somewhat better represented in part-time jobs, especially in television, but males still dominate in all areas.

Not only do men dominate what are often called the key creative occupations, this is also where the highest proportion of men in private sector broadcasting work. Forty-three per cent of the men fall into the semi-professional and technician category, compared to 21 per cent of the women. Meanwhile, half of the women in broadcasting do clerical work. **In other words, most of the women in broadcasting are not doing what we associate with broadcasting work.**

Within the private sector, women are least well represented in the production segment, where most of the films and videos are made. Here women make up just over a quarter of the labour force. And this labour force is highly segregated, with most women doing traditional jobs near the bottom of the hierarchy. In a production manager's view,

hair, make-up, and wardrobe are still traditionally dominated by women and grip and electric is still dominated by men. And in production areas it is about fifty-fifty and the only one that is still the female domain is the production office, co-ordinators and secretaries. That's a bad area. Those people are underpaid and those people are overworked and that is definitely because they are women.

The data largely support her claims.

Over 70 per cent of the hairdressers and three-quarters of those in make-up and wardrobe are women, while well over 90 per cent of the grips and electricians are men. And 90 per cent of the production secretaries are women. The women who do make it into male areas are often segregated in terms of kinds of productions. According to a woman set decorator,

There's only about four or five women that work in [this city] as set decorators and a lot of them work as assistants and stuff like that. And still most of the men do the big pictures. They're all men. There's no women that really do the big pictures, there's no woman that really gets a chance at the really big films that come into town.

The production manager was less correct about the equal sharing of production work. In 1989, women were half the unit and production managers. But women constituted only 29 per cent of the producers and 16 per cent of the directors. They did, however, account for 41 per cent of the third assistant directors, a fact that reflects their low status given that this is generally a gofer job. Like women in the public sector, those women who make it into private sector production and direction do not have an easy time. Indeed, the focus on profit may mean the men making the decisions are less willing to take a chance on women.

They are not producers or directors but women producers and women directors. They represent all women producers and representing all women puts an additional strain on women in an already stressful job. Another independent producer is

very aware of being a woman ... with now a male crew. I don't think they do very much to give me the gears on that level but I feel a great responsibility not to dither or not to be intimidated and not to live out their worst expectations of us ... I try very hard to represent all of us, when I'm in difficulty, which puts me in difficulty, in even that much more strain and stress.

According to a highly successful producer, women are given no margin for error.

I mean ... that a guy director is allowed to make any number of mistakes if he's good on the gift of the gab and he's got a lot of confidence and he's in there kicking. He's going to keep directing. But I think if a woman makes a mistake, that's it. She's out.

Women do seem to find it easier to be writers than to be directors or producers. Over a third of writers available for production jobs are women. This may be partly accounted for by the fact that this work makes it easier for women to fulfil their domestic responsibilities, to combine their two jobs by working at home. As a writer explained,

certainly there are deadlines and sometimes you do have to work evenings and sometimes you have to work on weekends to make deadlines, so on and so forth. But it's much more flexible. I can be home for dinner, you know. I can see them [the children] in the morning and I can see them in the evening.

This does not, however, mean that women find it easier to get jobs or that they do not face barriers similar to women in other areas.

Women also do better in the art department than in either production or direction. But men still have two-thirds of the jobs here as well. And they do better in editing than in production, direction, or art. Women are, however, significantly more likely to assist the editor than to be the editor.

Many of the women who work in the private sector do freelance work and these women may well be more segregated than women who are regular employees. In NABET's two Canadian freelance locals, women represented only one-quarter of the membership and half the women are concentrated in the traditional female areas of make-up, wardrobe, hairdresser, continuity, and office work. These were not exclusively female categories, however, and, even in these women's fields, men may well be doing the most prestigious work. Although at least one man could be found in all but the apprentice editor category, there are no women in 12 categories, including such traditional male jobs as carpenter, electrician, boom, director of photography, and production designer.

Overall in the private sector, as the production manager quoted above made clear, **women are concentrated in areas where they are least likely to be involved in actually making films and videos or in determining which ones are made.** Indeed, in spite of the fact that women have more of the jobs – and more of the key creative jobs – in the public sector, such patterns of segregation are found throughout the entire entertainment industry. Moreover, the figures provided above may overestimate the extent to which women are actually involved in making films and video, given that they reflect the numbers available to work.

The 1988 Department of Communications data on Certified Canadian Productions indicate that women got a smaller share of the work than their numbers would warrant. For example, women produced only 19 per cent of these productions but are listed as accounting for 29 per cent of private producers. They did 11 per cent of the directing but make up 16 per cent of the directors in the private sector; only 17 per cent of those actually writing compared to 38 per cent of those available to write. Like women in other sectors, women in this industry mainly do women's work and face tremendous barriers against moving into traditional male preserves.

UNEQUAL PAY IN BOTH PUBLIC
AND PRIVATE SECTORS

Also like women in other sectors, women in this industry are paid less than the men. An overall figure comparing wages is not easy to establish, but the data available indicate that the gap between male and female wages varies with sector, location, job, and unionization.

Again, women at the National Film Board seem to be in the best position. In 1988, the average salary for women was relatively close to that of men in most categories, although there were still sex differences in pay. Women technicians involved in shooting averaged only 62 per cent of the male annual income while women cinematographers and those on the scientific and professional staff made three-quarters of the male salary. Women in almost all other categories got between 85 and 95 per cent of the male annual salary, and none were paid more than men in the same jobs.

It should be noted that these figures do not include either part-time or locally engaged employees, who may face a much more unequal wage distribution. Moreover, these figures can be looked at another way, a way that exposes much greater disparity. While 62 per cent of the women earn less than $30,000 a year, only 16 per cent of the men earn less than this amount. And almost twice as many men as women made over $50,000 a year in 1988, in spite of the fact that the number of women and men employed at the NFB was virtually the same.

CBC also seems to have a relatively small pay gap compared to other sectors of the industry. A senior woman in the corporation had a simple explanation for this. The CBC "has always paid the same because it has always been unionized." Among the CBC's non-contract or permanent employees, women earned less than men in all but four categories and less than 4 per cent of the women held the higher paid jobs. Two of these higher paid categories included only one woman, and the 14 women in senior management who were paid more only moved ahead of men in the last three years. During the same period, the much larger number of women in middle-management saw the wage gap increase.

Here, too, the figures do not include the many women who are employed on a contract basis and therefore may underestimate the disparity. Women who have to negotiate a contract each time they are hired may be even more disadvantaged, especially if they are not part of a network that shares information on wages paid to men.

While non-contract women in senior management at the CBC were paid more than men, the *Statistical Profile* indicates that senior managerial women in private sector distribution were paid only 71 per cent of the male average annual salary. The *Profile* did find that women doing clerical distribution work were paid significantly more than men. But there were few men doing this work and all the clerical salaries were significantly less than those of either the female or male office staff at NFB.

Data on the full-time employment earnings in broadcasting indicate a very unequal salary distribution between the sexes. In 1988, men were more concentrated at the top of the income ladder and women more concentrated at the bottom. More than twice as many men as women were paid over $70,000 a year and three times as many men fell into the next highest income bracket. Meanwhile, three-quarters of the women, compared to two-thirds of the men, were paid less than $30,000 a year. And these data do not include those below the level of semiprofessionals and technicians, the levels where large numbers of women are found.

Data on salaries in private sector production are difficult to find. The figures collected for the Toronto Women and Film study provide only a rough indication of salaries but they do suggest greater wage difference between women and men than are evident in the public sector. Statistics Canada data for 1986 indicate that women sound and recording equipment operators make 72 per cent of the male wage; photographers and camera operators 75 per cent; writers and editors 73 per cent; producers and directors 83 per cent.[7] These data include both the public and the private sectors. Given the small gap reported in the public sector, the gap in the private sector must account for the greater gap found by Statistics Canada and must be greater than these numbers suggest.

For example, the many women who are involved in independent production so that they can "deal with things differently," make "different kinds of movies," because they are "terrified of losing control and losing my voice," often make "a horrible living." One producer incorporated to protect "my three t-shirts and my kodiaks and my bicycle." Or as an independent film-maker in the Black community put it:

I love the independence [but] you have to take the responsibility for not being rich and famous ... when things get rough, I think, oh my christ, I'm 45, I don't have a house, I don't have – nothing and that's very frightening sometimes.

The data on private sector production also suggest that, among those eligible for union membership, the wage gap is significantly smaller for those who belong to a union than it is for those who do not. A senior woman who began in the private sector maintained that the "only reason my salary at some stage became equal to my male colleagues was because I was in a union shop and I participated actively in that union." According to a woman who operates a camera, "as soon as you are unionized, you are into ... [an] equal pay situation."

Most of the figures provided above relate to non-contract employees. The data collected by ACTRA provides some indication of what happens to writers and performers who work on contract. While women received 38 per cent of the contracts awarded in 1985, they accounted for only 20 per cent of those paid $35,000 or more. Moreover, no women performers or writers outside British Columbia, Ontario, Quebec, and Newfoundland fell into this income bracket, while the only exception for men was in the Winnipeg writer category. Women were also underrepresented among those with contracts worth between $25,000 and $35,000, given that they were awarded a mere quarter of them. They did, however, get 39 per cent of the contracts worth less than $5,000. Moreover, these figures may hide significant differences related to age. According to the ACTRA union president, "at the age of forty in performing in this country, women's incomes decline to well below the poverty line, whereas men's incomes soar from forty and beyond."

Also left out of these data are those who get no income at all. A camera operator "worked for free on two feature films"; an assistant editor was asked "if I wanted to come and work for free for a few months ... he said if I wanted to do that he would train me in director skills and from there he would recommend me for my first job." According to an independent producer, there are

an incredible number of young women who are hired in the lowest positions, for the shortest amount of time and often have their wages deferred, often work a hundred hours a week, often work at the leave of sexual preference ... they're extremely young, they're inexperienced, they're usually quite smart and they get ripped off.

Another producer had a story that supported this claim.

I thought I'd die when they paid me $200 a week to work around the clock, seven days a week and I thought they're gonna pay me too! When I was interviewed, I forgot to ask how much. I was just so keen on getting the job and there was the production manager, with his boots up on the desk and his cowboy hat on the back of his head, and he mentioned to me, "And yeah, we are also going to pay you." However, of course, at the end my pay cheque never came through.

Even experienced women can be caught. A freelance sound recordist "accepted terms of deferred payment and to that point had been doing quite well and was never paid and didn't work for a few months and ended up going bankrupt.''

At first glance, women in television and film seem to do better than women in general who average 66 cents on the male dollar. But, given the nature of the work that most women do in this industry, a more relevant comparison would be the average income of women in male-dominated professions. In 1980, women in such professions averaged 71 per cent of the male income. Given women's relatively recent arrival in these jobs within television and film, an even more appropriate comparison would be women in the younger age group. Women aged 25-34 averaged 77 per cent of male income.[8] **If these figures are used, women in this industry do not fare better than their counterparts in other areas and many do worse.** In any case, it is clear that women earn less than men, and some, at least, are not paid at all.

GOVERNMENT INVESTMENT

Telefilm
An examination of funding given out confirms the suspicion that men get more public money than women in all areas. Telefilm Canada is part of the public sector, but it works primarily with the private sector. Because Telefilm's job is investment in feature films and television shows, the critical question is who gets the money from this public sector funding agency? The numbers vary with year, type of production, according to whether or not women work with a man. But the short answer is fewer women than men and fewer women directors, producers, and scriptwriters than their numbers in the industry would warrant. And women have a better chance of getting money if they work with a man.

In 1987-88, women producers in the English sector accounted for only 13 per cent of the Telefilm-supported projects and more than half of these producers had a male partner. Women producers did better in the French productions but they were even more likely to have a male partner. Most of the male producers, on the other hand, either had a male partner or worked alone.

In the same year, women directors did slightly better in the English productions than either English producers or French directors. Yet almost three-quarters of the productions had male direction. And while women make-up more than a third of the writers in private sector production, they constitute just over a quarter of those writing in Telefilm productions. In the English productions, women are more likely to work with men than alone or with other women. Men were also much more likely than women to get jobs as performers and when there was a single lead, that lead was seven times as likely to be male rather than female.

Interviewed about the Toronto Women and Film study, Telefilm information officer David Ellis said: ''There's always going to be some old boy's network ... If most producers are men, then most of the money will go to men.''[9] Even if the producers are women, they may need a male for legitimacy. A highly successful woman producer reported that "it was very difficult to get people to take a chance on me. And in fact they wouldn't until I brought on, you know, a recognizable, bankable, male producer." The statistics suggest that this is not an isolated incident.

Provincial Funding Agencies

The patterns are similar in provincial agencies. In 1987-88, female producers received 16 per cent of the funds from the Société de développement des industries culturelles du Québec (SOGIC) and accounted for a quarter of those receiving funds. In contrast, male producers got 82 per cent of the funds but made up only 71 per cent of those participating. The rest of the money went to combination teams, and their share was relatively close to their numbers.

Female writers did somewhat better than female producers. They collected 23 per cent of the money and made up 24 per cent of those funded. Male writers' share of the money was very close to the proportion participating. In the case of writers, it was the combination teams that did well in relation to the numbers receiving funds. However, union membership lists of the Syndicat des techniciennes et des techniciens du cinéma et de la vidéo du Québec (STCVQ) indicate that 86 per cent of those doing scripts are women, suggesting that writers too are significantly underrepresented in relation to their numbers.

In Ontario, teams that included both women and men had the greatest success in receiving money from the Ontario Film Development Corporation (OFDC). Half of the combination teams applying were successful, compared to 40 and 41 per cent of the male and females applying without a partner of the other sex. Women were as successful as the men in getting some money but they received less money than their male counterparts. In 1988-89, female producers got only 3 per cent of the production funds while males were granted 52 per cent. Women received 13 per cent of the development funds, compared to 75 per cent for the males. And, although women did get more of the production funds than they had in the previous year (not a difficult feat given that they received no money from this fund in 1986-87), the reverse was the case in terms of development fund money.

Being female seems to mean, even in the case of the public sector funding agencies, less money for films. It may well be that the problem is more exaggerated when it comes to private funding agencies. According to one bank, they are currently funding only one woman producer and this is the first one they have funded.

Ideas about female capacities can have a profound impact on women's funding opportunities. Refused further funding by a provincial agency, a female director was told:

"c'est intéressant de voir ça dans le cinéma, les femmes sont vraiment bonnes pour l'organization ... c'était vraiment comme sous-entendus, c'est comme du secrétariat en quelque part, c'est comme les fonctions qu'on attribuent aux femmes, mais côté de la réalization les femmes manquent d'imagination, c'est les hommes qui ont l'imagination." Il m'a pas dit c'est ça ton probleme, mais il dit "les femmes manquent d'imagination" en me parlant à moi ...

SHOW BUSINESS

In many ways the film and television industry is an industry like the rest. But, also in many ways, there's no business like it. And many of the barriers women face are, according a senior manager in private television, "a function of the particular industry that we're in."

It is a male-dominated and hierarchically structured industry, where the kinds of characteristics usually associated with men are thought to be necessary to success. One independent producer summed up the industry in the following way:

I call it glitz. It's really defined the industry. It's competitive: it's hierarchical. With some exceptions, it's male. And it's extremely exclusive ... And they control the commercial aspects of the industry ... It's almost like movies are made on the notion of scarcity ... only a very few people get to make them. And only a very few people get to decide who makes them. And that creates in itself an economic scarcity and also the most dangerous scarcity, the scarcity of access to audience. And most of them are men.

Echoes of these words were evident in interviews with women throughout the industry. A sound recordist described it as "a very male-dominated industry. They have very strong, definite, aggressive ways in which the industry works," and a woman in wardrobe said, "I mean, it's a male-oriented business, so you have to understand that you're dealing with it all the time." Viewed from the perspective of a senior manager in private television, "it's hierarchical and unrelentingly so ... [a] business where pecking order means everything." or as male producer put it, "it's structured as a patriarchy"; an industry in which people have to be tough, take risks, display great confidence in themselves, an industry in which successful women often have to, as one such woman made clear, learn to "operate like a man." Indeed, the characteristics that are valued are those most often associated with men.

In spite of the pyramidal structure, however, there are few clear routes to the top or even into the bottom. For example, "anybody can be a casting director if they so like to put out their shingle. There's no casting director school ... somebody turns around and says, 'I'm a casting director.' It's those kind of things that are uncertain in the job." Similarly, there's no school for set decoration. You don't go to university to become a set decorator. Everybody goes to film school to become a producer or director, you know, or a cameraman. Nobody ever goes there to be an art director. Nobody ever goes to be a set director or a propman or a grip.

Although film schools primarily train people to be managers, directors, or producers, most of those who are in directing, producing or even managing did not get there by going to film school. On-the-job training is critical and, in the words of an editor, "there is just no trial in the film industry; there is no trial situation here. Either you are making a film or not."

The absence of clear career routes and the limited training opportunities that lead directly into appropriate jobs means that a great deal depends on mentors, personal choice and circumstance. In interview after interview, women and men talked about the problem of getting the first job and the importance of luck, timing, and, most important of all, personal contacts. According to a senior manager in private television, "it's getting into those conversations or getting access" that is the most critical hurdle in this industry. It is the networks that count, often even for union jobs. It is, in many ways, a patronage system.

This dependency on networks and on personal contacts is reinforced by the fact that it is also a fragile and ephemeral industry undergoing constant change. A male producer explained that it "is a pretty fluid and to some degree ... unstable industry in terms of getting work. It's a simple matter of who gets the job and who doesn't. Me is a pronoun that shows up a lot."

This instability, combined with the power of those at the top, means in the words of one woman writer, "you can change one person at the agencies and you'll find the answer going from yes to no." For many women such as one currently working as a production manager, this means "you're as good as your last job, and you have to keep on finding new ones, which means that you're constantly selling yourself."

But even being good at the last job does not guarantee the next job. Demonstrated skills and successful productions do not necessarily mean that subsequent jobs are automatically yours. In an independent producer's experience,

It's not a free marketplace where your show got good ratings and it was made on time for the right amount of money, therefore you get the job. Some of the producers who are succeeding are the ones who have had one failure after another.

And some of the women who fail to get the next contract have been very good at their jobs. At least that was certainly the experience of a woman producer who had a very successful film but had to struggle for financing on the next.

The need to seek funding for each project, another characteristic of the industry, contributes to the instability of employment and, according to some, to male dominance. "A lot of control in our business has to do with the selection of projects. What gets made, what gets funded, what gets shown, what gets distributed," according to the chief executive officer in a film company. Just as hiring is explained in terms of talent, funding and other support is explained in terms of the "quality of projects," as a person from Telefilm made clear. It has to be judged a "do-able banking deal," the bankers say, especially in the private sector, and a project that can sell.

Nobody wants to take a chance on a newcomer, male, female, or animal. They just don't want to take a chance. You got a lot of money at stake ... but if you're good you get work because in the commercial end of the thing, the world is amoral. They are not anti-woman, they are only pro-money. You deliver the goods in commercial terms, they won't care who you are. So on that side of things, value will prove itself.

This came from a man who should know, given that he is a senior executive involved in decision-making about films in the private sector.

The industry is also unlike others in terms of the hours and the demands on personal resources. A producer and manager in the private sector explained that

in the manufacturing process of motion pictures and television programs, one of the things that would restrict membership to women is the physical taxing that goes on. To make films is a very demanding discipline physically.

The way production tends to be done in this country, it is a business that has "very long hours, always very stressful." There are 14- or even 24-hour days and weekend work is common. Hours are not only long, they are unpredictable, and sometimes require moving from place to place.

That it is "a very personal business" means not only that contacts count. It also means that people work under very intimate conditions with each other.

[It's] really top ended male-wise ... I want to say it's all sexual but maybe it only feels that way ... It's highly flirtatious if it's a predominately male crew with young – this is a cliche – young female production assistants and there's much flirtation and one has to be very centred in that atmosphere.

Like this actress, women throughout the industry talked about the "intimate relationship" of working on a set, the environment created when people wander about scantily clad, the close community that develops on locations.

A "very personal business" can mean as well that age and looks are factors in hiring. "Well, I know that women got jobs on crews [because] clearly someone thought they were cute and gave them a job." It is probably the case, as others claimed, that it's not cute but talent that allows women to keep a job in the industry, but cute may well be important in gaining that all important initial access. And it may not only be a question for women who appear before the cameras. Applying by phone in response to an ad, a woman who now works as a grip found the production manager ''was more interested in the facts about how old I was, how available was I, and what did I look like.''

The male-dominated structure of the industry and the assumption that the traits usually associated with men are required, the instability and reliance on funding combined with critical decisions based on ideas about quality, the importance of contacts and mentors in gaining access, the hours, the stress and the personal nature of the work affect everyone in the industry. But these characteristics of the industry have a particular impact on women and make it more difficult for them to enter, to stay, and to succeed.

The Male-dominated Structures

The male-dominated structure means that it is not only more difficult for women to get in but also more difficult for them once they are in the industry. Many women work in male-dominated structures, but the problem is exaggerated in this industry because so many of the jobs have traditionally been done by men while none of them have been exclusively done by women. It's hard, as a male decision-maker put it ''imagining [women's] capabilities in an area they haven't worked in before.'' Some men – and it is mainly men who make the decisions – think women camera operators ''can't carry the cases''; women directors ''can't control the crew,'' women producers ''can't handle money.''

Women's problems do not disappear with their first job. In a woman director's experience,

especially as a woman it's harder to break down the barriers and almost everything that I've done, every show I've worked on, I've been the first woman that's ever done it and there is a sense of, that therefore, it takes a lot more energy to get there and I'm hoping that then people will give other women a chance.

Many women have to continually be pioneers and to work alone with other men, in a male culture. To understand women's discomfort, a senior manager suggests imagining

if the tables were totally turned, every business situation that you [walked] into, every board room ... all your colleagues were always women and then a man walked into the room. It's easy to see when you think of it that way ... the tension level goes up.

Another woman director emphasized the importance of this male culture:

I think that it's one of the last bastions of male chauvinism. I think that the people who have the power are more comfortable dealing with women that they can dismiss or divorce ... I think that maybe one of the reasons that there aren't a lot of women directors yet is that the people that do make those decisions ... are men and feel more comfortable dealing with men, believe that being a director is like being on the front line of a battlefield. It's like you're shooting and taking shots, literally. And they don't think that women have the stamina or the whatever to be on the front line of the battle field. I know myself that I've lost a couple of pictures because they thought I couldn't camp out in Africa for two months, so it went to a guy ... I think that maybe that's why its harder for women, maybe that what they're doing all the time is making up for it, making up for the fact that you're a woman ... that whole thing that a woman has to be twice as good to get where she is.

Women have more trouble getting hired because the men who make the decisions often don't think they can do the job and once they do get the job, "if a woman makes a mistake, she's out." "The quality of the work, the standards that women have to make, are much higher than the standards men have to make in order to advance themselves," said a woman producer. Or, as a male producer put it, "they're given the opportunity primarily to fail."

While the problem is sometimes obvious, as in the case with the director who said to a female producer: "I won't work with a split-assed female," it tends to be less direct and more difficult to establish. For example, a woman in television drama talks about male assistant directors who found various ways to be unsupportive. "They can help with the crew or they can kind of sabotage you and it is very subtle." A producer described how a male director "deliberately slowed down the work." A woman editor sees

it more these days as a kind of glass ceiling thing. It is subtler, the barriers. And I think where it is extremely difficult for a woman is the camera department. And I honestly think that some of that is physical. Those 35 mill cameras are huge. But it is also something to do with not quite having enough faith in somebody who doesn't weigh 250 pounds and is 6 feet tall.

And it is frequently hidden by what is often called a discrimination-free emphasis on confidence, aggression, toughness, and risk taking. As a male manager put it, "if you're tough and your strong, you can win ... believe in yourself." From a film editor's perspective, however, these kind of criteria are often neither sex-blind nor even necessary."You don't really get considered for the big jobs. You don't. It is the commanding presence that they look for. I don't have, I don't think I particularly need [it] in the editing room." Similarly, a production manager did not think the tough manner of proceeding was essential to the work.

You go into a meeting with eight guys and all their trying to do is outmanoeuvre one another. It has nothing to do with the decision that has to be made for the movie. It's just jockeying for position, and that's really not a very constructive thing and it happens a lot. I don't think women do that and I don't think they could afford to. They certainly don't when working with men and, of course, when men are working with women, it doesn't make any difference to them.

Instability and Reliance on Funding

The instability and reliance on funding, especially when combined with a male-dominated funding process that makes judgments based on perceptions of quality, can also work to the disadvantage of women.

As a woman writer explained:

the gatekeepers are largely men – the decision-makers in the funding agencies, the producers. Therefore, I think what appeals to them is a different sort of thing than a lot of women want to write. I think a lot of women are writing and succeeding at it, but I think there are a lot of women who are not getting ahead because of the kind of thing that they want to write is not what men read. Not something that men identify with particularly. To quote from my own life, I've written a script which is a thriller but which has, as its central character, a woman ... and there is involved a best friend – a male best friend – and a private investigator and the husband. The number of men that I have had say, "Well, it's an interesting story but it ought to be about ..." And they seem to be very evenly divided as to which male character it ought to be about ... Probably a half a dozen men who have seen it, at least, have said, "But it ought to be about somebody else.

A male decision-maker confirmed that certain kinds of productions are favoured, at least in the private sector.

From my vantage point [it] seems to be that the women who are making it as directors in film tend not to get excited by creating and producing action adventure drama. Action adventure drama happens to be the most popular by virtue of who rents what types of video, who goes to see what kind of movie ... Women tend not to pick the hard commercial genres to prove themselves in, where men tend to do that.

Some women did report feeling uncomfortable about working on, or had even refused to work on, "jiggle shows" or episodes that "seemed to be merely an excuse to show young women being murdered." But it is not clear that the preference for certain kinds of action films are the only kinds of films that have a commercial value. At least one distributor suggested that other kinds of films would sell if they were funded. Indeed, some of the recent successes have been films that could not be called action adventure. What is clear is that what constitutes quality and what constitutes popularity are not objective decisions but rather are value judgments. And when it is men who make the funding decisions, it is men who are more likely to be evaluated as producing quality work that will sell.

That males make decisions about funding and hiring is particularly important in such an unstable industry because women are constantly having to be hired anew or funded again. This means that they are constantly having to prove themselves and establish the value of the work. If women often have to do this on male terms, it is a added disadvantage.

Education, Networks, and Mentors

There are schools for filmmakers. There are courses in technical areas such as sound and camera work. Schools and unions both assist in job placement. There are also some government programs, like Futures, that pay young people to learn on the job. All help women get into and stay in the industry. But unions are not always equally accessible to women, and the post-secondary education courses are not equally distributed between the sexes. Moreover, although post-secondary courses certainly lead many to jobs in related fields, formal programs are not the way most people enter the industry. As a result, there is a heavy reliance on networks and mentors. And this reliance often serves to discriminate against women.

As is the case throughout the education system, women's enrolment in post-secondary film and broadcasting courses appears to be increasing. They made up approximately a third of the graduands in 1990. Given that women constitute the majority of those currently enroled in all post-secondary programs, however, these figures indicate that women remain significantly underrepresented in courses preparing them for work in the industry. Moreover, these numbers may represent only temporary gains. According to one faculty member, "when I was teaching in the art school ten years ago, I would have ten women and ten men in a class. This year I have only three women and the other eight are men."

Access also varies by province. Approximately two-thirds of those graduating in film and television went to school in Ontario. But women seem to account for a larger share of enrolments in the other provinces that offer courses. For example, women were close to half of those in film/broadcasting courses in Alberta. While women seem to have a better chance outside the Ontario core, they had no chance at all in the Maritimes, because there are no programs offered there.

As is the case with getting jobs in the industry, entrance into programs does not mean that women have an easy time. The overwhelming majority of faculty are male and this too means a male culture. This culture not only affects students, it has an impact on faculty as well. Speaking from experience, a former teacher explained, "the number of women who teach film is appalling ... we're going into male-dominated departments, and male-dominated fields, and there's absolutely no support for us to be able to function in effective ways once we're in." Once female students leave the program, they may find even less support. According to this same faculty member, "right now when young women leave school, there's a vacuum, it's a pit, it's an abyss." There are few recognized routes into and through the industry.

Unions can help women get jobs, especially in the technical fields. And unions do help ensure that women get decent wages and conditions once they have a job. But some women find it difficult to get into unions. "I did try to join unions. I tried to join all the unions that are affiliated with music and with filmmaking and I never had any success," said a woman who works in sound. Another woman "found my way barred into the union because I was a female in a non-traditional job." There are a variety of unions in the industry and some have made it very difficult for women to join. This is particularly problematic when unions have an important voice in hiring. Some unions have allowed women to join but have not made many efforts to defend the particular interests of women. In a production designer's view, however, as women increase their numbers in unions, they are changing them. A woman in continuity described how the union was good not only for benefits, pay, and getting jobs but also for providing courses to acquire or improve skills.

Unions and schools help but mentors and networks are critical in gaining access, receiving on-the-job training, and moving up the hierarchy. Women and men who were interviewed talked about the importance of mentors and networks. Given the dominance of men in the industry, it is not surprising that many of those women who have made it have been helped by a man. Equally unsurprising, however, women also reported that men often feel more comfortable hiring men and that men have greater access to the all important networks.

Women producers and directors are frequently excluded from these male networks. An independent producer explained:

They're in sports together, they're in the locker room, the bathroom, and they exchange tidbits of information. They have access to this information, little bits of behind the scenes information of what's going on in different organizations, in the business in general. Women are barred from that. They are being barred from a lot of social life too ... particularly if you are a single woman. If you invite that man out to dinner ... where two men might do this ... [it] would be inappropriate, would be considered sort of a come on ... You don't have access to the sports communication, behind the scenes thing.

Lack of access can mean no job.

Many men in a position to hire may simply not know about the women working in the field. As one of them said, "I would assume that there were – certainly are – fewer women available to me in terms of the technical crew talent pool here than there are men for positions like gripping, gaffing, sound, camera, and the like."

The importance of networks and the limited formal routes into jobs can mean that women outside the Ontario industrial heartland or in at the early stages of development in particular kinds of productions may have an advantage over other women. For example, a woman who got her start in the Maritimes felt "in Toronto, I wouldn't have had the opportunity." Another now in a senior position was convinced that she was able to move because she was there when her branch was in its infancy and male patterns had not yet developed. But cutbacks in all areas, especially in regional centres, could mean these routes are increasingly closed to women.

A Very Personal Business

When you throw 60 strangers or 60 part-time freelancers together on a film set for 14 hours a day and it is hot – you dress for the situation – it is natural human nature to be attracted physically and I think that the worst part of it is that people react negatively.

According to this male producer then, the industry creates situations that encourage men to make sexual advances. The problem, as he sees it, is that many women object to these advances, defining them as sexual harassment. This man denied the importance of sexual harassment. Another denied that sex played any role in the business. The notion of the casting couch "is bunk. We may as well be manufacturing socks here," he claimed.

Almost all of the 50 women interviewed for this study had either been harassed themselves or knew someone who had. Their stories range from the young woman who went for an interview that turned into an attempted seduction, to the make-up artist who was threatened with firing, to the writer who quit after her boss introduced her to his couch, to the producer who lost a job when she refused to share a hotel room. Many of these stories are difficult to prove because they often amount to not being hired and because, as a filmmaker explained, "usually harassers don't do it in front of an audience." The dependency on the personal choices of those doing the hiring and the instability of the industry, combined with the concentration of women in the least powerful positions, makes women particularly vulnerable.

Equally important, and equally difficult to establish, is the sexist atmosphere that makes women constantly uncomfortable. Women reported dressing to try not to be physically attractive, ignoring the constant jokes, fighting the assumption that they slept their way to the top, being called "sweet cheeks," being asked, "What's wrong, have you got your period?" and avoiding obscene things written in public places. While most of these women say they simply try to ignore this atmosphere, it can have an important affect on the confidence that is so critical to success in this industry.

Conversely, more women in charge can ease the tension and counteract harassment. According to a senior male in funding, when it is women

who are in ultimate positions of power in individual film projects ... you'll find that in those situations, the issues of politics, harassment, however they get expressed, will become way less dominant, they won't be accepted, they just won't be part of the conversation.

A number of women reported that this was indeed the case. Women in senior positions find they are less likely to get harassed and others find they are less likely to allow harassment. Women can provide "a wacky kind of support" and a different kind of atmosphere. "I've had the rare experience of doing two various little films directed by women," said an actress, "and the entire feeling on the set was palpably different. Fascinating, as much of the predominately male crew allowed their softer side, their gentleness, to come through."

The Hours, the Location, and the Stress

A senior male manager in the industry offered the following advice to women: "Try to keep your personal life at bay and then decide I'm going to be a filmmaker." Would he have offered the same advice to a male? It seems unlikely. As a woman production manager explained, "There are a number of men who work at production managing who have wives at home who just do the wifely thing. But I don't think that situation exists for women or necessarily do women want it to exist for them."

The hours and the unpredictability, as well as travel that is part of the work, makes it much more difficult for women than for men or for women in other industries to have a family. Unlike the men, many of the women stay single. According to Statistics Canada, 42 per cent of the female producers and directors, but only 30 per cent of the male, are single. Compare this to the labour force as a whole, where only a quarter of the women and 30 per cent of the men are single. This is not simply the situation of women at the top. Among radio and television broadcasting equipment operators, 45 per cent of the women are single compared to 36 per cent of the men. As a drama director explained, when it comes to a career and a family, "it's a lot harder for a woman to have both than it is for a man ... A lot of my women friends who are producers are not married and don't have children and don't have families either."

The women who do have both often find it very difficult. As a sound recordist put it, "this industry is very tough on relationships." But it's harder on women's family life, especially if they want to have children. According to a woman producer, "it's very different to be a mother of a four-month-old boy and to be producing a film than it is to be the father of four-month-old boy and producing a film." A woman in continuity found that "women still carry more of the burden of raising children and also proportionately the guilt when they are away so much." Children are a problem for women even when women work at home, as another producer testified.

The other difficulty is that you need to have time to work. You need to have time sometimes to yourself and that is not possible sometimes. For instance, I'm working at home; [her son] is home all summer. I'm doing both things, helping him to remember his schoolwork and whatever and I'm working at the same time. And frankly, sometimes there is a lot of screaming because I'm up to my ears ... A woman can't do anything if she has more than one child.

In the words of another producer, men "are more likely not to have a child, even if they are fathers."

Women make all kinds of adjustments in order to juggle their two jobs. They work at home, often switching to writing or other work that need not be done away from the children. Some refuse work that involves an extended period of time or a different location. Some drop out all together for a period of time. Some move out of the creative jobs into management so they can have regular hours. All these strategies can have severe consequences for women's careers, because they frequently move out of those all important networks.

Other strategies are possible, however. Although an actress lost one film because she was pregnant, another producer figured out ways that allowed her to work. "When he found out I was pregnant and [he] couldn't have cared less ... I was noticeably showing for a scene. He just sat me on the floor for this dinner scene and said 'oh ... we are there in New York. We'll all eat around the coffee table.'" In other words, he worked out a way to disguise the pregnancy and continue the film. A woman producer, who thinks "it'd be incredibly difficult to be a mother in my situation if I didn't have the situation I have," had managed to "have the self-confidence to turn around to my colleagues or to my crew ... and say, 'okay, guys, you're on your own for a while, 'cause I'm going to nurse my baby at lunch time you know.' The crew called it the milk run." A production manager suggested that other schedules are also possible. "I always hear that over in Europe about how they like to shoot a seven-hour day. That would make a big difference, but a basic shooting day here is twelve hours.'' Many women also manage because they have supportive partners and can afford to pay for help.

All these strategies suggest that it is structures, not women or children that are the problem. Women in the film industry are not the only ones who face long hours and shift work. More flexible and affordable day care centres could alleviate many of their problems. Similarly, women in the industry are not the only ones who suffer from the long and irregular hours of the business. Both women and men would benefit from a reorganization of work schedules that accommodated their personal lives.

While women continue to bear the greater burden of child care and guilt, men are increasingly parenting alone. As one single father described it,

I suffer in comparison to my colleagues because I have kids and I refuse point blank to miss a baseball game my son is in or a soccer game my daughter is in, in the name of some silly dinner with some potential investor or some dopey colleague who wants to do this or that.

Men are often in a better position to make these choices, given their location in the industry. However, it is clear that the structure of the industry hurts both male and female relationships and that adjustments could be made to make family life easier for both sexes.

CONCLUSION

In the late 1980s, women were nominated for, and won, Genie awards in film and Gemini and Gemeaux awards in television at rates that exceeded their share of jobs in the industry. Women have also been well represented in film festival nominations and on festival juries, although the numbers vary with the festival and are still less than the number of men. Only in Alberta were women underrepresented as jurors, nominees, and winners.

In terms of specific categories, women did very well as directors, producers, screenwriters, and art decorators in the Gemini awards, here too winning awards in excess of their share of the work. This was also the case in the art decorator category of the Genie awards. Women were nominated in the Genie producer and screenwriter categories in numbers slightly below their representation among job holders but they were not represented among the winners. Nor did any women win in the director category of the Genie awards, even though a significant number were nominated.

Women are winning these awards in spite of the odds. Women in the film and television industry are not only in a worse position than men; they are in a worse position relative to women in the labour force as a whole. Their share of the jobs is significantly less than women's share of all jobs. They are more segregated than men and hold fewer of the most senior and creative positions. In almost all job categories, their income is lower than that of men and it is sometimes non-existent. And they receive less funding than their numbers warrant. Women face a male culture in an unstable industry where traditional male jobs predominate and where quality is defined primarily by men and determined through the funding process. These conditions contribute to the sexual harassment and the unfriendly atmosphere that many women face and make it very difficult for them to have a family life. Moreover, cutbacks in state financing are likely to undermine the gains women have made in the public sector and the recession to increase the competition from men in the private sector. Women, as the last in and least likely to be full-time employees, are undoubtedly suffering from the current reductions in public financing.

There are reasons for optimism, however. That women have made the most progress in the public sector, where equity programs have been introduced, clearly indicates that such strategies can have an impact without destroying the quality of the productions. Moreover, the very instability of the industry means it is possible to introduce change quickly. According to a man from Telefilm, "good ideas, smarts, forcefulness, etc., [have] perhaps more possibility for women than other more traditional occupations ... It's less institutionalized." But smarts alone have not been enough for women. As a woman who records sound put it:

because of the fact that there aren't many women in the industry in the higher, more powerful positions, I think they get less recognition as a result and so it's like a vicious circle in a way. The person who wants ... the job ... gets turned down because they don't have enough experience but can't get the experience without getting the job.

Getting the job and getting the funding requires positive action for women.

NOTES

1 / Over 50 men and women, representing all kinds and levels of industry occupations from both the private and the public sectors across the country were interviewed for this study. Their words add flesh to the statistical bones found in *A Statistical Profile of Women in the Canadian Film and Television Industry*, Project Report by Peat Marwick Stevenson & Kellogg (Toronto: Toronto Women in Film and Video 1990). Although some of those interviewed were willing to have their remarks attributed, others were not, and I therefore decided to treat all in confi-

dence. I would like to thank Susan Crean and Diane Silverman, who did most of the interviews, for their help.

2 / *Statistical Profile*, Employment, exhibit III-1. This document examines women in the industry in the following categories: employment, earnings, government investment, education and training, and awards; unless otherwise stated all figures come from this report.

3 / Ibid., exhibit III-4a

4 / [Francine Fournier and Bonnie Diamond], *Equality and Access: A New Social Contract* (Montreal: National Film Board of Canada 1987), 30

5 / Ibid., 36

6 / Ibid., 26, 44

7 / Statistics Canada, *Canadians and their Occupations: A Profile, Census 1986* (Ottawa: Supply and Services 1989)

8 / Katherine Marshall, "Women in Male-Dominated Professions," *Canadian Social Trends* (winter 1987), 11

9 / Quoted in Julia Nunes, "Women Underrepresented in Film Industry, Study Shows," *Globe and Mail* (Toronto), 10 March 1990

Part Two   COMMENTARY ON THE ISSUES
           BEHIND THE NUMBERS

MARGARET VISSER

2 Breaking the Frame

The dramatic arts (of which radio, film, and television are modern varieties) always reflect society to itself; they respond to social attitudes and seek to influence them. The production of spoken and enacted communication is of necessity a joint enterprise, requiring cooperation from large numbers of people, all of them performing separate but complementary tasks. Social prejudices and changes in social structure, therefore, are also expressed in the very organization of the team working together to inform, stimulate, flatter, or persuade the public. As in all work forces in our society, coordinators of the team become leaders and authority-figures; only a very few people, and not necessarily the most talented or least replaceable members of the group, become celebrated or publicly honoured.

In the historical beginnings of Western theatre, in Athens in the 5th century B.C., women were almost certainly never allowed even behind the scenes. "Society reflecting itself to itself" meant men speaking; female characters appeared in the plays, but they said what men gave them to say, and men, dressed as women, said it for them. Women were so undervalued in 5th century B.C. Athenian public life, in fact, that we are quite surprised to hear that they actually sat in the audience and watched the plays. They emerged from private life sufficiently to step out onto the stage, in theatres of the Western world, only centuries later.

There are ancient social prejudices against women venturing at all into the public domain, and to this day women often prefer to avoid theatrical life because of the necessity it imposes of working in public and in groups. They traditionally tend still to practise the solitary arts: novel-writing, poetry, painting, and sculpture. In these they can do what they like, when and how they like. In large stratified groups they cannot. Men in groups cannot do as they choose either: they too have to interact and submit to the problems of involvement with others. But women, in a group of mixed sexes, are still at a disadvantage in comparison with men – collectively, automatically at a disadvantage. They are likely to do the menial work and the temporary or dead-end jobs, and to be paid less than men are, even when they do work that is equally important. We – both women and men – are only just beginning to perceive the injustice and the waste caused by this ancient and blindly defini-tive classification.

A document like *A Statistical Profile of Women in the Canadian Film and Television Industry*, then, is a sounding of society in general and not merely of its own industry. Drama, in the broad sense that comprehends film, television, and broadcasting, is still the image – even behind its scenes – of society itself; it is, furthermore, a microcosm of the segment of society that is supposed to hold its most "advanced" ideas.

A preliminary point must be made of the recurring complaints from the compilers of the *Statistical Profile*: that severe limitations are placed upon its scope by a simple lack of data.[1] The issue is raised, for example, of the extent to which women participate in projects financed by public funds – but the same question is not asked of private funding. Is private funding, one wonders, necessarily more risky, less amenable to controls, less subject to surveillance, less confident in women's abilities? We cannot pursue the matter because there are *no statistical data* on it. Similar reservations are found to be necessary throughout. It is clear that further research is necessary, and that ways must be found to encourage film and television companies to keep data that note the gender of their employees. Such a practice would, apart from anything else, be a consciousness-raising exercise.

We see from the evidence that has been collected (primarily from the public sector though it is) that the situation of women in television, film, and broad-casting has been steadily improving in relationship to that of men. The gap between women's and men's pay in these industries is smaller than that in other workplaces.[2] However, the numbers of women in these fields are lower than the national average (43 per cent for all industries, 35 per cent for film and television); and women remain underpaid in all the categories investigated in this study.[3] In order to look at why this should be so, we have first to realize that two main kinds of disadvantage exist: societal ones, the product of the social system and of the mind-set of the people already occupying the field; and internal ones, determined by women's own perceptions and their ideas about what they can and want to do.

People intending to learn and to increase their capabilities usually, and quite sensibly, begin with what they already know. In the world of film and televi-sion, women's jobs tend, naturally, to be traditional: women are to be found in clerical work, wardrobe, hairdressing, and makeup. In other areas they often exercise skills which develop from ancient expectations that women must be good at housekeeping: they work as continuity staff, set supervisors, assistant camera crew. They keep tabs on things, put them away where they can be found again; they maintain order.

In the very beginning and at the very bottom of the hiring scale, a traditional – and literal – male *forte* most probably skews women's choices and opportunities: heavy machinery – cameras, props, packing-cases – are most likely to be easily lifted and moved about by men, so men are expected to handle them. Women generally have better-tuned fine motor-skills, and more precise finger movements: they gravitate (have *traditionally* gravitated) towards typing, telephone operation, filing, office organization. They provide in the private sector of these industries 90 per cent of secretaries, 93 per cent of script supervisors and continuity staff, 85 per cent of wardrobe artists.[4] The trouble is that heavy machinery is needed on the shooting-floor, and office-work is necessarily walled off from studio work. And it is in the studio and on the shooting site where drama actually takes place, and where creative skills in the field are learned. Women should beware of being "streamed" as secretarial staff or as cleaners and tidiers. Secretarial positions, for women interested in moving into actual filmmaking, might be embarked on in the first instance as temporary, with written assurances that experience can be gained away from the office desk, either during tenure of secretarial work, or later. There must be *conscious* opposition to what is, after all, a universal tendency: to categorize permanently, to live only up to expectations, and to settle into inertia.

Even if we hypothetically accept the status quo, however, questions arise from the documents before us. If women's traditional skills are what women are allowed and generally prefer to practise, why, for example, are women so under-represented in television programming for children? Producers of films for children in English, funded by Telefilm – admittedly the overall sample is not large – are 76 per cent men, and only 8 per cent women (the rest are a combination of men and women); directors 77 per cent men and 23 per cent women, scriptwriters 78 per cent men, and 22 per cent women.[5] Telefilm allocated only 7 per cent of funds to women for children's productions in English. Men, of course, can know as much about children as women can, one is not denying it – but we are here discussing *traditional* roles; and men have clearly collared a good deal of the market in this traditionally "female" sphere, if we remember that 35 per cent of the workers in the industry are women. Men are even preponderantly represented as *performers* in what is created on the television screen as typically a child's world (55 per cent men, 41 per cent women, the rest unknown in English; 60 per cent men, 30 per cent women, 10 per cent unknown in French). It would be interesting to find out how and why this happened. Could it be that men are simply cast more often, as well as more often as the protagonists, in programming for children, on an analogy with their more frequent casting, and casting as heroes, in films for adults? If the impression given by the data is correct, then children's programming is an area where women could profitably concentrate more of their energies in future.

Women, again, are supposed to be good at handling people and to perform well in situations involving interpersonal relations. It is clear from the figures that the most successful women in the field do become producers and directors, jobs requiring social skills and leadership capabilities of a high order. But women work often *in cooperation with men*, even to the point of preferring to apply for grants and to present projects as part of a team that contains men.[6] Women are 13 per cent of senior producers at the Association of Television Producers and Directors of Toronto. They are 29 per cent of producer/directors, 16 per cent of directors – and 60 per cent of associate producers. Women reach the top *echelons* alongside and supporting those in charge, but they actually fill the role of "boss" substantially less often then men do. In other words, it looks as though women's 'cooperative" skills are taken advantage of, rather than set free to be used creatively, or in the service of whatever goals women set themselves.

Most women working in directly creative positions in television, radio, and film "stand behind" and help men, or work in partnership with them rather than alone or with other women; men are still apparently expected to be, and expect themselves to be, more assertive, to take more initiatives, to "stand out" more than women do. All this is understandable, given women's upbringing, but it is culturally determined and unnecessary; the point is now commonly accepted. We have, as a society, begun to work on undoing such conditioning; we have still a long way to go. What is less often remarked is the unfortunateness – the injustice but also the wastefulness – of our propensity to undervalue people, whether male or female, who support others. Supporters of either gender are utterly necessary and often irreplaceable, and should be valued and paid as such. But since the very word "support" suggests a position "lower" than what is supported, such a role tends – entirely mistakenly – to be devalued in a competitive system.

A disquieting suspicion is that even women who have been freed from a good deal of the old conditioning play supporting roles because they shy away from the "top" places. They *can* take top positions and receive top pay for them – they often do, but it may be that they prefer to play safe, doing without the limelight and the pressure and thereby avoiding risk. Apparently women ask for smaller sums of money than men do, and also receive "significantly smaller dollar amounts than men and combination teams" do.[7] Women seem to be more cautious than men about launching into expensive projects – in part, no doubt, because they are less likely than men are to be entrusted with large sums of money by investors. It is disturbing, for instance, to learn that as the value of employment contracts increase, women are awarded fewer of them. In

1987–88, women received 9 per cent of total Telefilm funding for production; men got 76 per cent and combination teams 15 per cent.[8] Here we touch on a huge double-bind that will dissolve only with time and experience: women remain on the whole less confident in their abilities than men are, and (therefore) other people are less confident in them.

It is utterly unfair that women should have to "prove" themselves and "be better than men" in order to be given an equal chance to succeed. But this is a period of transition, where "ought" is still a luxury; women *ought* to be given the benefit of the doubt, but they cannot expect to be given it until the doubt becomes smaller. It *is* being steadily reduced; but meanwhile women, whether they like it or not, have a duty to other women and to history to do their part in reducing what lack still prevails of confidence in women as performers in public life. In other words, every woman who can, should. She acts not only for herself but on behalf of others – men as well as women.

To return to the conventional picture of men of muscle and women of precision: if the schema represents any truth at all, and even if it is nothing but a convention, it offers an advantage for women, which they have only to seize. Technology forces the post-industrial world to be more and more precise, more skilled at detail and at intricacy – at work that far more closely resembles embroidery than digging ditches. If everything were working within traditional models and *justly* within them, women would out-perform men at technological expertise.

Nothing could be further from the way things are. Nowhere are women weaker in the field than at straight technology: at shooting film, maintaining equipment, managing machinery. Art directors are 29 per cent women; photography directors are only 1 per cent women. "The job category in which women earn the least relative to men is 'shooting.'" And things are getting worse in the "professional," "semi-skilled manual" and "manual" groups in the private sector.[9] Technology remains a male preserve. Women are most probably scared away from it from an early age; it just never becomes, for most of them, an option. This is in spite of the traditional view that women are good at finicky and precise rather than hefty work. It must be that women are *culturally* turned off, intimidated through socialization. They then become oddities if they try to enter fields of technological expertise.

One of the difficulties is undoubtedly the group of male guardians a female must encounter and win over before she can reach almost any machine. A camera crew is an especially clear example of this phenomenon. They are a team, and they already know both each other and what to do. In an already constituted group of males, a female can be an intruder and a potential disrupter of the group's complex and delicate structure. For a woman to become part of such a working group, to be allowed to work "hands on" with the group's members on their precious machinery, requires courage on her part and extraordinary openness and civilized generosity on theirs. Men "not letting women in" to all-male configurations such as work-teams is an exceedingly soft option for them; they can relax into a culturally induced stereotype that offers them security in power. "Men in packs" is said by anthropologists to be one of the oldest, most atavistic of human groupings. Even on this front, women and men are showing that working together is not only possible but rewarding – yet we still have a long way to go.

Film schools are increasingly turning out female graduates: more than one third of the students in 1989-90 were women; two years previously women had been only 22 per cent or less than a quarter of the total. Women must educate themselves to specialize in the field, that is obvious; and film schools must work on placing their graduates in the industry. Education is not everything, however. More and more women are taking film courses, including those teaching directing skills, yet women generally "represent significantly fewer" directors than their proportional representation in film and broadcasting courses would lead us to expect.[10]

As directors, Quebec women do outstandingly well: for example, the Association des réalisateurs et réalisatrices de films du Québec reports that 28 per cent of film directors are women; Telefilm funds went to women directors in the proportions 22 per cent of French feature films and 25 per cent of French television drama, as compared with the figures 19 per cent and 7 per cent for English language production.[11] Are French Canadian women doing well in this area because the industry as a whole is freer there from the tyranny of "big bucks"? Is it because of a French tradition of respect for relatively independent, director-conceived, low-budget art films? It would be interesting to know.

Women tend to fill part-time positions and term contracts; there are fewer of them within than outside the industry's unions.[12] It is important to discover whether women's lives, their "fit," for instance, within the family and their husbands' career patterns, compel them to accept temporary and part-time work, or whether there is a discriminatory factor here (influenced no doubt by expectations that a woman may not put her career first), setting things up so that women *can only achieve* temporary or part-time employment. And where women's numbers are unusually high in top jobs in the profession (for example among CBC producers and directors in New Brunswick or Ontario) are these women employed full-time or on contract? [p. 39] It is possible for women's advocacy groups to work out solutions to such problems – but only when the facts have been ascertained. The search for more information must include careful and detailed interviews with women workers themselves; counting people and comparing salaries is useful, but – even when the numbers collected are large – it can give only a limited perspective.

Women are exerting their greatest creative forces in short films and documentaries. They were producers on 59 per cent of shorts in 1987-8 for the National Film Board, and this increased to 76 per cent in 1988-89; allotments of funds to women in documentary climbed from 25 per cent to 43 per cent in the same years, and in shorts from 59 per cent to 76 per cent. Manifest success in these areas is encouraging whichever way we look at it. But the concentration of female talent in projects that are "experimental" rather than "mainstream," and which involve far less money and personnel than drama or feature films, may be typical of women's caution – and may also be read as a prejudiced lack of investors' confidence in their ability to take on and carry to completion very large and expensive projects.

On the other hand, the experience gained here can only improve women's confidence in themselves – which is at least as important an asset as confidence placed in them by monied interests – and will demonstrate to the world what they can do. Documentaries are a satisfyingly didactic medium for women who have messages to impart and protests to utter; they are also at present – perhaps because women are taking such an intense interest in them – an outstandingly healthy and lively art form.

In the last five years women have made undeniable and impressively rapid progress up the ranks of the hierarchy of the film, television, and broadcasting world. Nominations for prizes and successes in competitions demonstrate that they do receive recognition for excellence.[13] But the *Statistical Profile* makes the important point that women, in order to move closer to parity with men, and for the sake of the general health and truthfulness of our society, really must become "part of the group of people who decide what we can watch on television and in our cinemas " (p. 1); they must also be well represented in the "creative core" of film and broadcasting: as producers, directors, associate directors, writers, art directors and full (rather than assistant) editors.

The heartening fact remains, however, that it is surely women who at present have the most urgent and original things to say. The world has heard comparatively rarely from women in the past; and when modern women do give true artistic form and expression to their experience, the results are electrifying. A film director recently pointed out in an interview that, because women have, historically, been prevented from making their thoughts and feelings publicly felt, the dramatic climax in a film made by women often comes when at last a female character decides to speak out.[14] It is my conviction that in Canada the audience is hushed and waiting. Women owe it not only to themselves and each other, but to the whole human race and to its future, to use the media and speak out in their own unmistakable voices. Women, these days, have a corner on the best material.

NOTES

1 / *A Statistical Profile of Women in the Canadian Film and Television Industry*, Project Report prepared by Peat Marwick Stevenson & Kellogg (Toronto: Toronto Women in Film and Video 1990), see 1, 2, 11-12, 14, 19, 51-2, 95, 97, App. A-1

2 / Ibid., 10, 116

3 / Ibid., 10, 52, 113

4 / Ibid., 7; see also p.8 where 92 per cent of office jobs at the National Film Board are held by women.

5 / Figures in this paragraph are from exhibits III-11 and III-12, and pages 7, 9, 66, 70.

6 / Ibid., 47, 38

7 / Ibid, exhibit V-4

8 / Ibid., exhibits III-14 and V-1

9 / Ibid, 30, 40, 55

10 / Ibid., 95-6

11 / Ibid., 15, but see app. A-6; exhibit III-12

12 / Ibid., 20, 24

13 / Ibid., exhibits VII-1 and VII-2

14 / L.F. Miller, *The Hand That Holds the Camera* (New York: Garland 1988), 7

SUSAN CREAN

3 Culture, Gender, and Power: A primer on sexual politics in Canadian film and television

I HISTORY, HERSTORY, AND CORA HIND'S LEGACY

The history of women in broadcasting and filmmaking is not new or even relatively recent. It goes back to the beginning in both industries as it does in print, the medium that created the mass audience in the first place and gave it national and international dimensions. It is, however, an uncertain history. Being largely unwritten, it is largely unknown; being herstory, it is typically left out of official accounts. But it is there nontheless, a continuous presence which begs the question why talent, diligence, and the achievements of women have not counted for more.

One recognizable pattern emerging from the historical fragments is this: as the century delivered one astonishing mass medium after another – film, radio, television, computers – women were never included in the planning. Those who rushed in to organize each successive innovation were men who naturally created systems and programming in their own image and according to their own interests. The contemporary accomplishments of women were ignored, and each time women had to start again at the bottom, break into the field, and shoulder their way up the hierarchy making do with lower pay and fewer opportunities along the way.

There was a moment in the early days of television, for instance, when women knew as much about the new medium as men did, and had just as much experience with it – which is to say, none. Yet women producers and editors in radio and newspapers were not drafted, as their male colleagues were, and, consequently, did not participate in the development of television as they could and should have. It wasn't as if they were absent from editorial and middle-management ranks – though it is true they weren't to be found everywhere or in large numbers. In private radio they remained scarce as hens' teeth, but at CBC radio they had achieved some distinction. In the talks and public affairs department women programmers actually formed a majority after the war and, by the early 1960s, had risen to senior positions. The head of daytime information programming was Helen James who had sucessfully launched radio's first magazine format show ("Trans Canada Matinee") and one of CBC television's longest-running programs, "Open House" (later "Take Thirty"), which for years was the only place in Toronto where women were hired as television producers.

Television was not only established by this time, it was in the process of transforming North American popular culture. Within the CBC, television had assumed the bulk of the budgets and all the political weight while radio was given a bureaucratic back seat. It was, moreover, generally understood among the senior women in radio that the men running television were unsympathetic to the work they were doing. James was the first to quit. Her resignation in 1965 moved the CBC's president, Alphonse Ouimet, to pay her a personal visit to ask her not to go. He did not, however, offer her another job or talk about her future, when, at that point, she had been doing the same job for 13 years. A stream of talented women followed James out the door. Stymied by the growing prejudice around them, they chose not to acquiesce but to take early retirement or a chance on a second career instead.

With 30 years' hindsight, we can now understand this was not simply a case of radio being muscled into an inferior position and rendered less significant by television, it was also a power play between men and women. Television assumed the public spotlight; it was brash, new, and exciting, and it was where the men wanted to be. It became the sought-after medium of the moment, and radio, by contrast, was reduced, eclipsed, and effeminized. From a slightly different perspective, the change might also be seen as the action of a beleaguered elite retreating to higher ground, an adult version of the schoolyard classic where the boys gather up their marbles and move the game elsewhere, where the girls can't join in.

Another pattern the herstory reveals is the early establishment of women's programming – the women's pages in newspapers at the turn of the century, the women's interests and *émissions féminines* departments at CBC/Radio Canada in the 1930s. This dedication of space to the female perspective was originally a progressive, even radical, idea, for it represented a move out of the private into the public realm, gave women a voice in the public debate and, at the same time, a place to congregate within the profession. At times, then, these pages and programs have functioned as bastions providing training and opportunity not readily available to women elsewhere. But, inevitably, without a sustained effort to integrate women into the profession, the bastions turned into ghettos, and became career traps. Integration was not what was originally contemplated, of course, but this did not prevent women from using the situation to give each other a leg up. But that is all they could do; they could not transform the industry or convert the men and the mentality running it.

One clear demonstration of how such a transformation takes place is the story of Cora Hind, the first Canadian woman to hold a senior editorial position on a daily paper, who was made the agricultural editor of the *Winnipeg Free Press* in 1901. Hind went on to become a legend in her time, famed for her annual crop reports and harvest predictions. Much less well known is her legacy to women. When a vanguard of young women journalists appeared on the scene in the early 1960s, their early career breaks, in a startling number of cases, came courtesy of men who had started out at the *Free Press*. If they hadn't worked with Hind personally they had worked in a milieu accustomed to having a woman in a powerful leadership position. This meant they had professional experience of a capable newspaper woman which apparently made it easier for them to offer other women, even young women, opportunities and jobs. Hind's example opened up the possibilities for women mainly because she had taught a generation of men to flout convention.

II POLITICAL ACTION AND
THE INDUSTRY'S RESPONSE: THE SEVENTIES

The biggest change in the status of women in film and broadcasting has come about in the past two decades. In both fields, women are now taken for granted; their presence is assumed as is the possibility that those who choose to are able to pursue careers over a working life.

Reality, however, doesn't match that rhetoric, as the *Statistical Profile of Women in the Canadian Film and Television Industry* gloomily shows.[1] Many occupations are functionally off-limits to women: director of photography, construction co-ordinator, gaffer, grip, cable person, and senior management, for example. Their talents are circumscribed in other ways too. Women actors are forced to withdraw into minor parts just as they reach the height of their creative powers as they approach 40; visible minority women have to face restricted access to funding and limited opportunities in the mainstream. Inside and outside the mainstream, women are culturally marginalized. Ambitious young women are exploited by producers who offer them the "opportunity" to work without credit and often without pay. And women of all ages experience the straightforward injustice of always being encouraged to take responsibility while rarely, if ever, being given authority to go with it. Predictably, some women have found their own way of assuming authority. Few have been able to finance their own autonomy by buying a television station, but many have opted for small-scale, independent freelance work.

Statistically speaking, the change has been modest but dramatic nonetheless. A 300 per cent increase of women in CBC corporate management between

1974 and 1985, for instance, still only produces 21 per cent, three-quarters of whom cluster at the bottom third of the management ladder, earning 86 per cent of the male salaries. Yet even this change did not happen by natural evolution. It happened because political action has at various times pushed and prodded the status quo, making an issue of the absence and silence of women. The report of the Royal Commission on the Status of Women set the stage in 1970, laying out the figures to quantify the underrepresentation of women in all walks of public life including television, and providing the arguments for policies, laws, and a radical shift in the state's attitude to women and work. The organized women's movement took up the case but trained its attention on the manner in which women are portrayed, and their bodies used, in television, film, and advertising. It developed an analysis linking sex-role stereotyping to the larger question of socialization, gender, and power. Subsequently, groups like the National Action Committee on the Status of Women (NAC) and the (now defunct) Women for Political Action wrote briefs and made interventions at hearings of the Canadian Radio-television and Telecommunications Commission (CRTC) during the 1970s; MediaWatch was set up during these years too, not only to monitor sexism in the media, but to orchestrate debate and public awareness around their treatment of women.

In the 1980s, the feminist critique of cultural norms erupted into the debate about pornography and violence against women. (Pornography being understood as the theory of socially sanctioned misogyny, violence and abuse the practice). Although television was implicated, Canadian broadcasters didn't blunder into the fray until 1983 when First Choice, the newly licensed national pay television service, announced it had made an agreement with *Playboy* to produce adult films. The idea that sexually explicit material, perceived by large segments of the population as offensive and degrading to women, was to be made for Canadian television with the government's approval and the public's money (through tax breaks) galvanized a coalition of women's and community groups, who took to the streets in several Canadian cities in a bitter February cold. The protest succeeded and the project was quietly dropped, but not before emphasizing how cravenly addicted commercial television is to sexism.

During these years the CRTC acknowledged the problem, but did little more than shake its head ruefully. In fact, the commission has proven to be spectacularly reluctant to do anything more than that. In 1979, after several years of lobbying by women, the commission launched a task force on sex-role stereotyping in the broadcast media which eventually recommended a two-year period of self-regulation by the industry. Broadcasters were left to draw up their own guidelines and comply if they wished. At the end of the trial period a national survey revealed such serious inadequacies that the CRTC was forced to conclude that self-regulation was ineffective and further action needed.

Since 1986, however, there has been a curious waffling back and forth: first the commission made compliance with the guidelines a condition of licence; then it approved the industry's proposal for a system of broadcast standards councils and agreed to lift the conditions of licence if broadcasters could demonstrate full participation in the scheme. Even while it was introducing a new regulatory instrument, the CRTC was contemplating ways to avoid using it, apparently hoping that the industry would come through so they could leave it to the public to enforce its own standards – policy by public complaint. For 12 years the CRTC has done its best to appear to be taking action leaving a paper trail of intentions as a monument to its own ambivalence. Late in 1990 a second national survey was released, proving once again that volunteerism doesn't work.

The portrayal of women *on* the media is, of course, related to the treatment of women *in* the media, but these twin concerns have never been successfully connected as matters of public policy. When the status of women in broadcasting was originally raised in the early 1970s, the response of the broadcasters was to adjust the picture slightly by putting women on-air where they would, of course, be seen. In 1974, the CBC took the daring step of having Jan Tennant read the Easter weekend news. This was considered an amazing event at the time, news in its own right, and the country tuned in to see if the world was coming to the end or taking a new lease on life. Indeed it was a symbolic moment, but it did not mean that women had arrived or that CBC management had seen the light. It merely confirmed that the question of women's presence behind the camera, in the back rooms and front rooms of editorial and managerial control, was on the agenda.

Over the next fifteen years there were major efforts at reform within the two oldest and largest cultural institutions – the CBC and the National Film Board. In the first instance, women in the CBC began meeting and pestering head office for a response to the Status of Women report. As a result, a task force was formed in 1974, headed by Kay MacIver, then director of radio for the English network in Montreal. The MacIver report was published a year later and was unequivocal: women's main frustration was due to the fact they were working, as MacIver said, in a man's world. What is fascinating about her document today is not the statistics so much as the attempt to elucidate the mechanics of discrimination, to isolate the attitudes that presaged the acts. After interviewing personnel officers across the system, the task force took the four most common stereotypes about women and checked them out against the real opinions, ambitions, and qualifications of women. Truth could only be found in the allegation that women were not qualified for some (technical) jobs; all the other chestnuts were devoid of any corroborative evidence, patently false, and often silly. It concluded:

Women in the corporation are treated inequitably as a group. It follows that individual women are frequently victims of discrimination since decision makers often make judgements about the capability of individual women on the basis of characteristics they associate with women generally, and act on these assumptions to deny women access to many categories of work.[2]

In 1975, the CBC head office set up an office of equal opportunity (OEO) to ensure that corporate hiring practices were corrected to prevent further injustice.

The OEO was very active in the first five years of its existence, but found all its efforts (policy, reviews, awareness seminars for women, "sensitization" sessions with managers and staff) had little impact. The results were so poor the executive vice-president was persuaded to include a equal opportunity objective in his 1980 annual operating statement. Had this been implemented, all hirings, transfers, and promotions would have had to take the goal of ending job segregation into account. But with the arrival of a new president, a change in government, and continuing rounds of budget cuts, it was soon forgotten. In any case, in 1983 a royal commission on employment equity was convened under Judge Rosalie Abella. Although Abella concluded, as the OEO had, that employment equity has to be mandatory, the Conservative government passed legislation in 1986 following the letter of her recommendation but rejecting her advice to accompany any program with tough enforcement mechanisms. The law, in fact, does not require companies or crown corporations to enforce employment equity, only to have a program and to report employment statistics to Ottawa annually. So the CBC was relieved of the obligation to enforce its own policy or heed its own experience, and the movement for reform was permanently stalled. In 1985 the OEO was closed and its director laid off.

Meanwhile, in 1974 the National Film Board (NFB) set up Studio D, an outgrowth of Kathleen Shannon's successful working-mothers series for the Challenge for Change program. These films had proven there was an audience for films made by women, and demonstrated that there are some films only women can make. Studio D has made a remarkable contribution to Canadian filmmaking. Its productions have won fame and notoriety on an international scale, and several (*If You Love this Planet*, *Not a Love Story*) are recognized as classics. Yet for all its Oscars and its success with audiences, Studio D has always had to fight for its existence and its budgets. Its status within the bureaucracy is never assured and it remains visible to the mainstream only when it suits. When the Applebaum-Hébert committee review of federal cultural policy published its report in 1982, the section on the NFB left women out of its account and, incredible as it may seem, ignored Studio D when it dismissed the board's output as "no longer represent[ing] a significant film experience for the Canadian public."[3]

In a larger context, we can easily understand why the only serious and sustained reform activity occurred in the public sector. For one thing, both the CBC and the NFB are unionized, and, being public institutions, they are susceptible to public opinion and political pressure in a way the private sector is not. Yet even with this strategic advantage it has been extraordinarily difficult for women to organize politically and maintain the effort. Partly this is due to the peripatetic nature of media work (erratic hours, travel), partly it's due to the reluctance of these professions, dedicated as they are to reflecting the world around them, to look at themselves critically. Significantly, the main effort of the 1970s was undertaken by ad hoc committees of women working independently, and it was not until the mid-1980s that unions and associations began addressing the question of women's status in the industry – or even breaking down their own membership lists. (The exceptions being ACTRA and the journalists union in Quebec. Even so, it fell to Toronto Women in Film and Video, another independent organization of women, to undertake the first comprehensive statistical profile of women in the business.

This history suggests the solution to the problem is not so simple and easy as setting up an OEO or a Studio D. Because the activism which produced these two projects was never formalized, both programs were endangered when commitment evaporated in senior management. Studio D remains the only woman-run filmmaking centre in the country and, as such, is the only place where women's work is given a place of privilege (as men's normally is, for example). But without other equality measures to support it, the haven remains isolated, a convenient excuse not to hire women or do ''women's films'' anywhere else. Moreover, while women in the CBC and private television can perhaps be faulted for not demanding more action from their unions, Studio D can be criticized for not being more accessible and supportive of independent and minority women filmmakers.

III WOMEN, THE ARTS, AND
CULTURAL POLICY: THE EIGHTIES

The political action of the seventies succeeded in defining the problem of employment equity and in extracting partial solutions from reluctant and dubious managements in the public sector. Private industry eluded the issue and, notwithstanding public criticism, has to this day not been required to take responsibility even for its pejorative portrayal of women. Set in a broader cultural context, though, the achievement of women in film and television is significant for they were the first in the cultural sector to engage their colleagues in the debate. The question of equality and creative opportunity is always an awkward and elusive one in fields which deal in images, ideas, and illusions, and which, moreover, are built on subjective judgment. Discrimination is often invisible to those experiencing it for it thrives on sins of omission rather than commission.

For many artists the creative challenge of the 1970s was, in any case, survival; the task at hand to assemble an infrastructure capable of producing indigenous Canadian work – books, magazines, plays, music, paintings, and performances. The political challenge was to promote cultural policies which would give proper prominence to Canadian art and would address the problem of a dysfunctional distribution system geared to the massive importation of foreign, mostly American, culture. Women were deeply engaged in both projects and it was 1978 before anyone in the arts stopped to ask the other question. It came in a report written for Canadian Artists' Representation/Front des artistes canadiens (CAR/FAC) by Ottawa artist Jane Martin who counted 28 women among the 229 jurors on Canada Council visual arts panels during the previous eight years. Was there a connection between the low number of women receiving grants and the relative absence of women on juries? Martin's study was instantly controversial; the visual arts officer denounced her and her report though he was never able to refute her statistics. But the idea was infectious. Other women began researching the worlds of literature, theatre, art education, video and filmmaking. The evidence accumulated that women do not have equal access to publication/ production and public subsidy, proving that in actual fact Canadian cultural policy does not benefit women and is not intended to.

The discovery was a rude one. Women were shocked to discover how low the percentages actually were. The rule of thumb, which is to say the best one could realistically hope for, was 30 per cent. (And 12 years later that ceiling has crept all the way up to 35 per cent.) In some fields (writing, for example), appearances had been truly deceptive, the numbers and visibility of practising women artists belying their real status. This, then, also showed how the nationalist movement had failed to mature and extend its purview beyond the interests of white middle-class men. Fifteen years of activism had produced official recognition of the nationalist argument in the Applebaum-Hébert report, but Applebert devoted exactly two sentences to the subject of gender bias in the arts, subtly misrepresenting it and lumping women in with other disadvantaged groups. "Arguments were advanced intending to demonstrate an underrepresentation of women artists, native artists and artists from various regions on juries, among grant recipients and among artists whose works are purchased by Art Bank."[4] No comment, no research, and check that word "intended." All the committee would concede was that jury membership ought to be rotated frequently "in order to counter criticism of favouritism." The idea that juries should reflect demographic diversity was overruled by an invocation to excellence (which "should be the only criterion for judging grant applications"), the old familiar shibboleth which had first been used against cultural nationalists.

The 1986 report of the Caplan-Sauvageau federal task force on broadcasting was the other key policy statement on culture in the 1980s. Here the issue of gender was at least dignified with a small subsection in the chapter on the principles and objectives for a new broadcasting act. Yet four pages out of 700 is not a lot of dignity, or evidence of serious concern.[5] The entire matter of sex-role stereotyping and systemic discrimination was collapsed into a few generalities and fatherhood recommendations. The portrayal of women was cast in terms of equality rights, which the task force proposed the CRTC worry about. Caplan-Sauvageau's retreat to a non-position was a huge disappointment to groups (MediaWatch, the Committee on the Mass Media in the Nineteen-nineties, NAC) that had hoped serious attention would finally be paid to employment equity, and to the proposal that a new broadcasting act contain an equity clause. (In the end it was Flora MacDonald as the minister of communications who was responsible for inserting references to gender in the principles section of the new act.)

The response of Applebaum-Hébert and Caplan-Sauvageau to the representations of women was, in effect, to deny them. The Canada Council's initial reaction had also been to deny responsibility, claiming it did not have the mandate to counteract discrimination or to give directives to client organizations to hire more women or to produce more work by them. Tim Porteous, the council's director in the early 1980s, disputed the analysis, maintaining that the real issue was the low numbers of women applying for grants. And, he added in an interview with me in 1984, "You cannot allege discrimination unless you can look inside the heads of the people on those juries."

Porteous was not the first or the last arts official to confuse the allegation of gender bias with an attack on artistic excellence, on the independence of juries, and ultimately on the integrity of the men (and token women) serving on them. All the same, he realized that records had to be kept, and the resulting monitoring process has (with help from unions like CAR/FAC, the Writers' Union, and the Playwrights Union) seen a steady rise in the participation of women. The percentage of women filmmakers receiving grants, for example, rose from 25 per cent in 1975/76 to 41 per cent in 1985/86.)

There is, in other words, a body of knowledge and experience relating to the status of women in artistic/creative professions that the film and television industries should draw upon. The first, most obvious, and easiest measure to adopt is parity on all juries, review committees, and boards considering film projects. The second is for a coalition of unions and associations to assume the task of monitoring the situation and providing the political weight and continuity to provoke and/or inspire improvement over the long term. Such an industry-wide grouping (parallels for which can be found in the Book and Periodical Council or the Coalition of Creators and Copyright Owners) could institute apprenticeship programs and should set up a grievance committee for women working in the nonunionized, independent sector.

IV WHEN THE POLITICAL GETS PERSONAL:
MEN AND THE STATUS OF WOMEN

In all this talk about equity, what tends to disappear behind the percentages are the real experiences of people – men and women. Both sexes are involved here, after all; both are implicated in the problem and essential to its solution. Thus far the industry and the men running it have not accepted the truth of the systemic discrimination which is responsible for the figures found in the *Statistical Profile*, much less their own role in it. As I have indicated, there has been an acknowledgment in certain quarters, and there obviously are cases of individual men who have taken on the issue and made a point of promoting women. But there has been no leadership within institutions, unions, production houses, or the industry as a whole, of the kind that would push the issue into the mainstream and make it a matter of professionalism as well as social justice.

On this score the response of the men interviewed for this document is instructive, representing a gamut from outright denial (that the figures in the *Statistical Profile* accurately depict the current situation; that discrimination against women exists in the business or that anything should be done about it) to a cautious recognition that there are gender barriers and that men can actually do something about them (such as refuse to serve on panels or juries which are not balanced; such as grooming women for senior positions; such as insisting on pay equity). Very few of these men had ever been asked to talk about the position of women in film or television before and most were uncomfortable doing so. Some were quite defensive about it and three senior executives requested that their female assistants also be interviewed, as if angling for a testimonial to their own good (non-sexist) behaviour.

There was, moreover, little in the responses to suggest that men talk to other men about sexism on the job or in the business, or recognize the role they play in determining the careers of women. It is unquestionably true that male behaviour (attitudes, beliefs, and well as actions) is the root cause of the inequality, yet men rarely perceive it that way. Unlike women, who have a keen sense of their culture and how they as a group differ in their habits, approaches, and ethics from the men they work with, men have almost no sense of belonging to a culture that can be called theirs. If ever there is to be a break through the glass ceiling and past the Thirty Per Cent rule to true equality, this will have to change. That is, individually and collectively, men will have to own male culture, right down to and including the really nasty part. Sexual harassment, for example, and the abusive exercise of power as exhibited in these stories.

ITEM   A production assistant with years of experience goes after a produ-
                         cer's job and is asked by her boss how badly she wants it. "A
                         single mother like you must be horny," he remarks while suggest-
                         ing she come around to his house on the weekend when his wife
                         will be away. She refuses and is not interviewed for the job. In the
                         grievance hearing that follows, management accepts the man's
                         excuse that he was "only joking." He is subsequently promoted;
                         she remains in her dead-end job.

ITEM   A fifteen-year-old actor on her first shoot is approached one night
                         by the production manager, who propositions her. She refuses; he
                         leaves a note pinned to her dressingroom door, which prompts her
                         to tell the third assistant director on the set, who in turn speaks to
                         her two male superiors. Neither man says or does anything.

ITEM   A veteran reporter applies for a job doing sports interviews at a
                         private television station and is asked by the producer to accom-
                         pany him out on location. On the way he stops off for a beer and,
                         when she excuses herself to go to the washroom, he interrupts,
                         saying they have to leave at once. In the car he becomes lewd and
                         suggestive, telling her she'll get along fine with the crew "espe-
                         cially on the road if you let the guys come to your room and tuck
                         you in at night." Finally he offers to stop at a gas station so she can
                         visit the washroom and tells her to take off her underpants in the
                         car so she can jump out quickly. Incredulous that this is happening
                         during a job interview, she fears the worst. Back at her own station,
                         badly shaken but unharmed, she reports the incident to her boss,
                         who tells her flatly she "must have imagined it."

ITEM   A woman is hired to do a technical job in an all-male shop. From
                         the beginning she is ostracized and, shortly after her arrival, some
                         of the men begin harassing her verbally. When it's decided she is
                         lesbian, the campaign becomes viciously homophobic; porno-
                         graphic photos are left in her work area. Eventually she complains
                         to her superiors and is advised to take sick leave. While she is
                         away, management circulates a memo to the unit saying that
                         discriminatory behaviour is not allowed and that anyone practising
                         it will be dismissed. This has the effect of turning the entire place
                         against her. When she returns the hostility is intolerable; she is
                         forced to appeal again to her superiors, but this time there is no
                         sympathy or support. Personnel has labelled her "difficult" and
                         unstable, the cause of her own trouble.

It is impossible to say how widespread sexual harassment is in film and television, but there is no reason to assume it is any less prevalent than in society at large, and some for believing the media's dependence on sexually based female imagery and its association with glitz, glamour, and ego encourages, even condones, sexist behaviour. The point is all women have to construct a professional self-image that takes their sexuality into account and allows for the possibility of sexual attraction becoming an undesirable element on the job. The unpredictable, untoward, and unsolicited in male behaviour is a basic fact in their lives.

One thing is clear: we cannot rationalize the extreme as aberrant or isolated behaviour. It is a part of a continuum which ranges from uncouth verbal chatter to violent physical or psychological acts of aggression. And it includes those on the sidelines who witness the incidents and choose to ignore or discount them or, worse, classify them as the private problems of the individuals involved.

The status of women in film and television is not a private matter, or even a women's issue. It is a public issue, a professional matter, and this means men cannot be passive observers. The pioneer women all got where they did because some man, somewhere, acted as sponsor or mentor. There may be more women doing the hiring now (and it could be that a major cause of the statistical improvement is the result of women hiring other women) but men are still instrumental, they still count in women's careers, and they are still (largely) in charge. The question is, will those who understand pass it on and will the committed lead the way?

NOTES

1 / *A Statistical Profile of Women in the Canadian Film and television Industry,* Project Report prepared by Peat Marwick Stevenson & Kellogg (Toronto: Toronto Women in Film and Video 1990)

2 / *Women in the CBC: Report of the CBC Task Force on the Status of Women* (MacIver Report) (Toronto: Canadian Broadcasting Corporation 1975), 69

3 / *Report of the Federal Cultural Policy Review Committee* (Applebaum-Hébert Report) (Ottawa: Supply and Services 1982), 263

4 / Ibid., 161

5 / *Task Force on Broadcasting Policy* (Caplan-Sauvageau Report) (Ottawa 1986), 143-44

LINDA SILVER DRANOFF

4 Strategy for Change

The data unearthed by *A Statistical Profile of Women in the Canadian Film and Television Industry* demonstrate that women are not receiving equal or equitable treatment as workers in the film and television world. Women in these fields suffer from inequities in pay, in employment opportunities, in access to government funding and to influential and powerful positions. Women do not affect creative program contents sufficiently, so their world view is too often missing from film and television programs. The data show that the situation is not improving appreciably, despite the existence of programs encouraging voluntary action.

The inequities confronting women in film, television, and video in fact mirror women's employment problems everywhere in the working world, so it is reasonable to suggest that the same factors that restrict women in one field exist in others. And the data in the *Statistical Profile* mirror the findings of numerous task forces and royal commissions which, from 1970 to 1990, have found that women are disadvantaged employees suffering systemic discrimination. This discrimination is linked to deeply rooted attitudes that prevent basic change from occurring. This situation is particularly damaging because the film and television industry is one of the primary sources of information, role models, and attitudes that impact on our culture.

The landmark Royal Commission on the Status of Women had confidence in 1970 that change was possible and could be implemented through "simple justice." In fact, over the years, government fact-finders and think tanks have worked towards change with thoughtful recommendations. A succession of politicians has promised improvements, and well-meaning legislation has occasionally been enacted. But most recommendations have not been implemented, progress has been limited, and women continue to be disappointed by the hindrances to their advancement.

Women's lack of progress is not for lack of effort or talent. Women individually and in groups have lobbied and expended amazonian energy seeking to influence decision makers to make the world a fairer place for working women. Yet the rights of women, in film and television as everywhere else, hang suspended, and women seem like puppets held by an invisible string, arms and legs flailing, dissipating energy without getting anywhere significant. It is my view that only strong laws enforced by government and backed by pro-active programs have any chance of improving the situation.

THE FACTS

At work, women essentially remain housekeepers and not "heads of household." The data in the *Statistical Profile* show that women not only continue to be denied employment opportunities and kept as subordinates within the film and television world, but that women's view of the world is not adequately reflected in programming.

Women dominate the supporting positions (production secretary, makeup, hair, and wardrobe), the clerical roles (women are 84 per cent of clerks) but are tokens in management and creative positions (9 per cent of managers, and 14 per cent of the influential creative positions). In the private broadcast industry, women represented 1 per cent, and in the Canadian Broadcasting Corporation, 23 per cent of the senior managers.

Women don't share fairly from the treasure chest of government funding. In 1987/88, women producers received from Telefilm only 9 per cent of their funding, and women directors and writers worked on projects that received 9 per cent and 15 per cent of the funding respectively.[1]

And women continue to be paid substantially less than men. In non-union technical positions, women earn only 67 per cent of what men earn (in all other fields it was 66 per cent). The few who make it to the executive level earn 97 per cent of what men earn.

Other surveys in related fields show a similarly unacceptable pattern: men outnumber women scriptwriters at the Canadian Broadcasting Corporation five and six to one (Actra 1982); 17 per cent of plays produced are women's (1988 Playwright's Union); 30.21 per cent of newspaper bylines were women's.[2] And in the United States, it's the same: Meryl Streep for the Screen Actors Guild recently reported that in 1989 women filled only 29 per cent of the movie roles and earned significantly less than men.[3]

It's not much different in totally different fields, where the Employment Equity Act 1989 reports revealed that women comprised only 481 out of 4538 managers in the public service, 58 out of 728 federally appointed judges, and 12 out of 211 directors on the boards of Canada's major banks. Federal employers, like the banks, broadcasting, transportation, and communications firms, crown corporations and agencies, have had a flurry of training and educational activities, but, according to the *Globe and Mail* on 24 October

1988, "that has not translated into real gains for visible minorities, women, the disabled, and aboriginal people" and "most continued to hire and promote white, able-bodied men for more desirable or better-paying jobs."

The pay situation for women in all fields is no better. Statistics Canada reported that women working full-time in all occupations earned just 66 per cent of what men earn, a marginal improvement over the 60 per cent ratio in 1970. It is interesting to note that in occupations classified by Statistics Canada as "artistic, literary, recreational and related," women in 1970 earned 69.7 per cent of what men earned; this improved by 1980 to 76.8 per cent, but by 1985 this had dropped to 75.8 per cent. This suggests to me that the trend to improvement may have stopped. Indeed, studies by Ontario labour economist Morley Gunderson have shown that at least 10 to 20 per cent of the disparity between male and female incomes can be directly attributed to discrimination.

Equal pay laws have not worked to improve the situation. Legislation offered hopes more than enforceable programs in their statements of principle that men and women should be paid equally, but did nothing to ensure that it would in fact happen. The Ontario Pay Equity Act of 1986 was the first legislation to be mandatory, pro-active, and results-oriented.

Women are, in fact, not improving their ability to remove themselves from poverty, according to a 1990 report of the National Council of Welfare.[4] In 1975 and still in 1987, 59 per cent of adults living in poverty were women. At the same time, the National Council of Welfare also called for the Canadian Radio-television and Telecommunications Commission (CRTC) to enforce its guidelines on sex-role stereotyping in the media to help women see themselves in non-traditional roles.

Reports on the status of women standardly recommend that the media be required to depict women less stereotypically, in order to help women break out of their preconceived conventional notions. However, it is those women who understand the destructive and limiting character of the stereotypes who must undertake the task. And unless and until those women break through significantly to senior creative and management positions in the world of film and television, it is less likely to happen.

THE HISTORY

The report of the Royal Commission on the Status of Women (1970) recommended the changes needed to ensure for women equal opportunities with men. The commission pointed to "overwhelming evidence" that inequality of opportunity for women is "widespread," and stated unequivocally that special treatment in the form of affirmative action programs would be needed to correct the adverse effects of discriminatory practices.

The commission also expressed concern about the stereotyping in the mass media, and that all provinces should prohibit discrimination on the basis of sex and marital status.[5] At that time, only Quebec and British Columbia prohibited discrimination on the basis of sex, and none dealt with marital status.

The commission recommended the appointment of advisory councils to government. Status of women councils composed of private citizens were then appointed in most provinces across Canada, leading women to hope that women's needs would be reflected in recommendations to government and in actions by government. However, in my view, there were not enough appointments of people with knowledge and interest in women's issues. Governments, in turn, ignored many of the important recommendations that were presented, and well-meaning women on these councils dissipated their energies without producing real social change. In some provinces and in the federal government, a minister responsible for the status of women was appointed within the cabinet. The Ontario Status of Women Council (of which I was a member) pressed for it, hoping that with an advocate within the decision-making structure, beneficial change would result. But the party system was our undoing. Women's needs kept being subordinated to the minister's priority of party loyalty.

In 1974 the CBC formed a task force in direct response to concerns expressed by women employees about the lack of opportunities. It reported that women in broadcasting did indeed have legitimate cause for concern, particularly in the area of job access. Fifty recommendations were made and some were implemented, including an office of equal opportunity, which was to monitor progress and hold attitude awareness seminars, briefings for managers, and career awareness seminars for women employees.

The CRTC got into the act in 1979, when it appointed a Task Force on Sex-Role Stereotyping, with representation from the CRTC, the public, the CBC, private broadcasting, the advertising industry, and the Canadian Advisory Council on the Status of Women. In its 1982 report, *Images of Women*, it made recommendations about sex-role stereotyping images in the media and employment issues. As had been recommended by the task force, the CRTC then monitored the initiatives taken by the broadcast and advertising industries during a two-year period and, in 1986, issued a "report on industry self-regulation." The report admitted, however, that it "contained no conclusions as to the effectiveness of self-regulation" but was instead "a progress report" from the perspective of the self-regulators. When the CRTC reported in December 1990 on progress, it concluded that little change had occurred between 1984 and 1988, that fewer women than men appeared in almost every area of Canadian broadcasting, that women continued to be portrayed in traditional roles.[6]

In 1980 the Ontario Status of Women Council submitted a report to the Ontario government on "Employment Strategies for Women in the 1980's" which recommended tough and wide-ranging measures to deal with inequities suffered by women in the work force. The report was not implemented by the Ontario government. The lesson I learned was that task forces, commissions, advisory committees, reports, and recommendations are often tools with which to avoid dealing with a problem, rather than a means of solving them. They are a source of change only if there is political will to make the necessary improvements.

In 1983 the Royal Commission on Equality in Employment, headed by Rosalie Silberman Abella, was established by the federal government to inquire into "the most efficient, effective and equitable means of promoting employment opportunities, eliminating systemic discrimination, and assisting all individuals to compete for employment opportunities on an equal basis" by examining the practices of government agencies and crown corporations, including the CBC. Its report, an excellent analysis of the problems wrought by inequality and the need for change, recommended changing the ambiguous and confusing term "affirmative action," which was "identified in people's minds with the imposition of quotas," to "employment equity." But the change in language has not yet been effective.

The report concluded that "voluntary measures are an unsatisfactory response to the pervasiveness of systemic discrimination in Canadian workplaces" and recommended "mandatory measures" with four alternative models for the government to consider. "Voluntary programs in the federal government," it said, "have had little impact on the composition of the public sector workforce."[7] The commission also disposed of the myth that public pressure would persuade companies to behave more fairly by calling it "unrealistic and somewhat ingenuous" to rely on public opinion as an effective monitoring agent." It recommended legislation to require employers to "take steps," to report progress annually, and to enforce equitable employment. If these measures failed, "consideration may then be given to the use of quotas."

Yet the Commission's recommendations were only selectively implemented, and the Employment Equity Act that took effect in 1986 was toothless. While employers were required to implement employment equity and file progress reports, the only penalty was for failure to file reports. Enforcement of employment equity was left to the Canadian Human Rights Commission to lay complaints at its own initiative if, on a review of the reports, it believed an employer had established or pursued a policy or practice that deprived a member of a protected class from an employment opportunity. The initial progress reports under the Employment Equity Act have not been promising.

This review of the history leaves the key question unanswered: why has the problem become so intractable? Why have women through history seen gains lost and the same tactics applied repeatedly to keep them down?

WOMEN AND POWER

Men remain powerful, despite twenty years of concerted effort by women and women's groups. Many men will not give up their power and many women accept it. Men resist change, not as an organized movement, but as a community of mutual interest, using teamwork. Men with power will try to find a way around any structure, any set of rules, to maintain their power, especially if compliance is voluntary. We should not be so naive as to believe that men will share power to be fair or even to be perceived as fair. Those with power do not give any of it up out of a sense of moral rectitude, or to avoid embarrassment and criticism, but only if the rules of the game unequivocally require it.

To some extent, men keep power because women let them; some women, for example, do not feel worthy unless a man considers them so. Women must stop looking for acceptance or validation primarily from the men, and learn to give validation to themselves. Otherwise, a successful woman will regard herself as an exception and may be less likely to make an effort to help other women to succeed. She may be less likely to sustain long-term success herself, for she will be the token who will be trotted out when the male power structure needs her credibility for their own purposes, but she is likely to be less accepted and supported within the power structure than the men are.

Men with power allow women to work, even to advance somewhat, but not to control the important decisions. When men decide who among our women is worthy of advancement, they sometimes choose the women who consider themselves "exceptions" (and therefore not representative of female talent), but who do not work for female advancement. As a result, the women who might create social change do not have the opportunities they should.

Sisterhood is essential if change is to be made. Women at every level of every working environment must make a special effort to work as a team and advance the cause of other women. We cannot expect men to hand the future to us. Women must be happy for other women's success. Individual women need other women's support, encouragement, and common goals to create and sustain lasting change. Individual women acting in isolation, applying all their energies to create change, will eventually burn out. Women will not succeed as individuals unless we all succeed as a group.

Power is partly a matter of choice; a woman has to make a decision to be powerful; she has to empower herself, and others she has the opportunity to help by mentoring. Individual women tend to blame their failure to advance on personal inadequacy instead of on systemic discrimination. In 1985 the Canadian Advisory Council on the Status of Women published *What Will Tomorrow Bring? A Study of the Aspirations of Adolescent Women*, which revealed just how unrealistic young women are. When young women were asked to anticipate problems they might have in the paid labour force, and specifically what might prevent them from promotions, 69.2 per cent believed it would be their own fault because they were "not good enough" or "not working hard enough," or because of a "personality conflict with the boss."

Women like to believe that qualifications and hard work are the key to entry to the better jobs. That is the myth of male advancement, and women think they can succeed by emulating it. Participation in training programs and working hard are useful, but they are not the key factor that makes the difference between success and failure for women. They may in fact be a delaying tactic. The emphasis on training and education for women is sometimes a way to put off real equity, to put the blame on women for their failure to advance, to ignore differential treatment. There is also the myth that women will become the economic equals of men if they can make the grade in the supposedly unbiased market economy. This theory assumes that men in power are unbiased and will permit market forces to operate freely when that option may not be in their self-interest. The reality is that the marketplace does not respond to reward women's work even when that work is in demand. Nurses, for example, are in great demand, but salary levels and working conditions have not responded to supply problems. As a result, fewer women are selecting nursing as a profession.

The main obstacle to women's advancement, then, is lack of power. Men resist sharing power with women. Although they let women work for them, they will only move over for women if forced. Even then, they will change the rules of the game so the arena vacated to women is viewed as relatively unimportant or second class.

At the same time, women cannot leave it to men or the marketplace or fate to empower them; they must validate and empower themselves. Women must work with and for other women and refuse the self-aggrandizement of being a token.

ATTITUDINAL CHANGE

A change in attitudes is essential but not easy. When decision makers make choices that exclude female advancement, it is often an unconscious response to their own comfort level and not intentional discrimination. People are more comfortable with a person who looks, talks, and acts like them, who laughs at the same jokes and lives a similar lifestyle.

By concentrating on programs to change women's attitudes, the established structure has evaded responsibility and in effect blamed the victims for their own victimization. Programs are required which work to change the attitudes and practices of the decision makers themselves, to make them aware of their resistance. That requires a massive educational "eye-opener" program to change the awareness level of the decision makers. The model for these novel programs might be the behavioural modification sessions given to the men who batter women. Male employers and supervisors who withhold fairness and advancement from their female employees are engaging in a form of mental abuse, which can be compared to the abuse of strength and authority exercised by men against women in the home.

Women in film and television have real power to affect how people think. For example, equality can be taught as a practical skill in the media by showing boys and girls sharing household responsibilities. Equal pay and equal opportunities will not be possible without an equitable division of labour in the household. Girls should see a broader life and career horizon to prepare themselves realistically for the world they will enter.

STRUCTURAL CHANGE

Employment equity must be institutionalized into the structure of our working world for there to be successful change. Programs to improve equity in the workplace are usually temporary, and excessive effort is expended on waging the same battles over again to justify the need for the program. Programs must be funded adequately, institutionalized as a permanent part of the structure, and withdrawn only if the need for them disappears.

The rules of the game must be unequivocal before men will cooperate in change. We must create a structure that is clearly defined, with stringent enforcement and penalty mechanisms, so that those in power will have no choice but to change or to suffer risks they will see as personally perilous. Compare the income tax rules, for example which most people follow because of the penalties imposed for breaches of the law. Managers should be held accountable for their failure to promote women in their departments, and their personal job evaluation, and therefore their own promotability and income level, should be related to their performance as promoters of equal opportunity.

Such a structure and clearly defined rules will provide some bargaining power to women. In the game of power politics, bargaining power is essential to negotiate change.

THE STRUCTURE MUST BE
MANDATORY AND ENFORCEABLE

Solutions have so far emphasized persuasion and voluntary measures, in the belief that companies and employers will be persuaded by "bad press" to behave themselves, and will willingly hand over power to avoid poor "public relations." There is also concern that powerbrokers will resist quotas, and that it is better not to get them angry and jeopardize their goodwill.

But these arguments are unrealistic. Self-regulatory models have not worked. Without mandatory programs, no significant change happens. Tough legislation, with mandatory targets and quotas, are necessary to achieve concrete results.

For example, the City of Toronto reported progress only after mandatory programs were introduced.[8] After 11 years of official effort to hire and promote women, they still make up less than 29 per cent of Toronto's civic workforce, and these advances mostly took place in the four years since the city established specific goals and targets for each of its 16 departments. In fact, the chief executive officers of every crown corporation canvassed by the Royal Commission on Equality in Employment acknowledged (p. 125) that legislated mandatory requirements were the most effective way to equity in the workforce. Similarly, the corporations that were successful in implementing employment equity advised that corporations must set targets, goals, and timetables if the goals were to be achieved (p.124). All agreed that a public reporting requirement was essential, but not of itself adequate without further legislation, particularly in a depressed economy.

STRUCTURES AND STRATAGEMS
Governments can make a difference through the enactment of policies, programs, and laws, provided the will to succeed also exists. The best solutions are pro-active programs that actively seek to achieve and ensure results, and that have enforceable remedies.

The Employment Equity Act
The Employment Equity Act passed in 1986, required federal employers of 100 or more persons to implement employment equity by identifying and eliminating employment practices that resulted in barriers against women and other designated groups (aboriginal peoples, the disabled, visible minorities), and by instituting positive policies and practices that would make their representation proportional to their numbers. In the communications sector, this legislation applied to the CBC, all radio and television stations licensed by the CRTC, cable television, and Telefilm.

Employers were required to make a plan, set out goals and target dates for their achievement, and file reports annually, or suffer a penalty of up to $50,000. The reports were sent to the Canadian Human Rights Commission (CHRC), which could, if appropriate, lay complaints of systemic discrimination. From the outset, however, the CHRC has criticized the act's weak enforcement provisions. In its first annual report, the commission stated that voluntary measures and self-regulation were unable to make substantial and unequivocal change. Bell Canada and the CBC are even challenging the power of the CHRC to base investigations on the statistics under the Employment

Equity Act. And it is reasonable to ask whether the complaints mechanism of the CHRC is adequate to redress systemic discrimination.

The Employment Equity Act must be reviewed in 1991, and women in film, television, and other areas must ensure that it is toughened up. The employment equity branch of Employment Canada is assessing the possibility of transferring enforcement to a new Employment Equity Commission and is preparing a report for the parliamentary committee that will review the legislation. If women want tougher measures, the 1991 review is a key place to start. Women should build coalitions with other women to ensure that this review meets the needs of women in every field of endeavour. Reports under the existing Employment Equity Act should also be sent to the CRTC to review in the context of licensing hearings.

The Charter of Rights and Freedoms

The Charter protects every person's right to equality without discrimination. This is not an active protection, but a statement of principle an individual can raise before a court in the context of a lawsuit. What the Charter does say is that every individual is equal before and under the law and has the right to the equal protection and equal benefit of the law without discrimination based on sex. It does not create an enforceable remedy, but only legally justifies affirmative action (employment equity) programs that actively try to improve conditions for disadvantaged individuals or groups. The Charter does not provide a methodology to create change, it just does not impede change. This means that mandatory pro-active programs with tough enforcement mechanisms can be enacted without any negative impact from the Charter.

Licensing and Broadcast Policy as a Means
of Promoting Employment Equity

The CRTC licenses public and private broadcasting, which, present legislation says, "should be varied and comprehensive and should provide reasonable, balanced opportunity for the expression of differing views on matters of public concern." The CRTC can review "programs and financial affairs or otherwise." It does not currently inquire into hiring practices of regulated companies. Present legislation relies on "moral suasion" and the licensees' "will to please us," according to a CRTC official.[9]

In a research study prepared for the Caplan-Sauvageau Task Force on Broadcasting Policy, authors Mahoney and Martin argue that section 15 of the Charter which guarantees equality rights for every individual can be used to justify regulations prohibiting stereotyping.

The task force considered whether this licensing role could be used to require licensees to promote equality, and concluded that the right to equality must be balanced with the right to freedom of expression.[10] It noted with approval the CRTC approach of self-regulation, which involves voluntary compliance by broadcasters with a code of ethics. The task force pointed out that this policy alone cannot guarantee equitable representation for women on radio and television, but that only increased participation of women in broadcasting will reduce the stereotypic portrayals. A Catch 22 – the solution is more women, but that is the problem too.

The task force recommended that broadcast licences should include an obligation to establish an equal opportunity program, which would provide for significant increases in the hiring of women and members of minorities in strategic positions. It also recommended that the government should appoint more women to the boards of the CRTC, the CBC, and Telefilm, and to other decision-making positions to reflect their relative numbers in society. As well, all broadcasters should ensure that women and minority groups have equal creative opportunities to produce and disseminate their works.

It appears these recommendations have not been implemented. There is little doubt, however, they would be helpful, in conjunction with mandatory measures. The new Broadcasting Act contains the promising statements that

the Canadian Broadcasting system should ... through its programming and the employment opportunities arising out of its operations, serve the needs and interests, and reflect the circumstances and aspirations, of Canadian men, women and children, including equal rights, the linguistic duality and multicultural and multiracial nature of Canadian society and the special place of aboriginal peoples within that society ...

[section 3(1)(*d*)(iv)]

and

the programming provided by the Canadian broadcasting system should (i) be varied and comprehensive, providing a balance of information, enlightenment and entertainment for men, women and children of all ages, interests and tastes ...

[section 3(1)(*h*)(i)]

Under the new act, the CRTC licensing power is quite broad. It is empowered to establish whatever conditions it deems appropriate for the implementation of the broadcasting policy stated above, which includes "programming and employment opportunities ... including equal rights." The act goes on to describe the regulations which the CRTC could enact but does not specify how the CRTC might direct licensees towards implementing equality in broadcast policy. The legislation should be amended to add to section 10 the following sections enabling the CRTC to:

1 / "make regulations ... respecting and prescribing the constitution of programming and advertising which would implement its broadcasting policy to "serve the needs and interests, and reflect the circumstances and aspirations, of Canadian men, women and children, including equal rights ..." and which would prescribe the manner of eliminating sex-role stereotyping in the media."

2 / "prescribe an appropriate manner of implementing equal rights in employment opportunities arising out of its operations, in order to serve the needs and interests, and reflect the circumstances and aspirations, of Canadian men, women and children.

As a result, the CRTC should be required to develop clear directives in the regulations. Women with an interest should be in communication with the CRTC to help them develop the appropriate guidelines. The manner of implementing employment opportunities could, for example, be a mandatory employment equity program with targets and quotas, and the penalties for failure to comply would follow the enforcement provisions of the act. The CRTC would have the power to make mandatory orders, or to take away licences or fail to renew them. A corporation that failed to comply with a regulation or order of the CRTC would suffer a potential fine of up to $250,000 for a first offence and up to $500,000 for each subsequent offence.

Contract Compliance

Contract compliance is based on the principle that companies and employers will not gain access to government contracts if they discriminate against women employees and do not take steps to correct the problem.

The Federal Contractors Program was passed as an adjunct to the federal Employment Equity Act. The program tries to enforce equality of employment opportunities by potentially withholding federal government purchasing power. In the program, companies with 100 or more permanent employees, which bid on contracts for goods and services of $200,000 or more, must certify in advance in writing that they will implement employment equity. Twelve hundred and seventy companies are now part of the program. Successful bidders are subject to review by Employment and Immigration Canada, which administers the program, and those employers who fail the review are banned from further bidding until recertified. Only two companies so far have been banned.

However, this program has limited usefulness for women in film and television, because the program applies to large-scale undertakings and most media efforts are on a smaller scale. But the concept is an important one, and an effective contract compliance program can be useful even in film, television, and video, provided it is tailored to the field. The paperwork required for participants in the Federal Contractors Program is instructive and can be utilized and adapted for any contract compliance program, even those on a small scale, as long as its enforceability is extended.

The concept of contract compliance has been insufficiently utilized in the film and television industry, considering the fact that government provides a substantial proportion of the funding. For example, the Ontario Film Development Corporation released figures in August 1990 estimating that Ontario's film and video industry benefits from approximately $550 million in public funding out of the national total of $1.2 billion.[11]

The principles of contract compliance could be brought to bear in funding decisions within Telefilm and the CBC, for example. CBC and Telefilm contracts could contain terms requiring producers to demonstrate equality in hiring at all levels of production. Telefilm already has an agreement with the government ("Memorandum of Understanding," April 1989), which, although it gives Telefilm the right to exercise independent judgment, imposes a duty on Telefilm to administer its funding "to achieve the cultural objectives of the Government of Canada," to "conform to the Canadian Association of Broadcasters Code of Ethics," to conform to the CRTC programming standards, to "provide employment opportunities to Canadians at all stages of broadcast program production," to achieve "linguistic balance" by providing at least one-third of the fund to French-language programs, and to achieve "industry balance" by using at least one-half of the fund for private broadcasters and/or provincial education stations.

There seems to me no reason why Telefilm could not also be required to achieve "gender balance" in the employment of staff at all levels of production and to strive for an absence of sex-role stereotyping. Currently, CRTC program standards are limited to controls on the display of violence and sexual exploitation. This should be expanded to include a reduction of sex-role stereotyping.

Pro-active programs and policies are not enough without sincere political will. We need politicians truly committed to equality. Women have had enough of broken promises and empty sympathy, of countless recommendations for government intervention which are ignored. We need action with integrity from people we can trust.

NOTES

1 / Unless otherwise stated all statistics are from *A Statistical Profile of Women in the Canadian Film and Television Industry*, Project Report by Peat Marwick Stevenson & Kellogg (Toronto: Toronto Women in Film and Video 1990)

2 / Data on scriptwriters comes from a 1982 survey by ACTRA, plays from a Playwright's Union 1988 survey, and on newspaper bylines from a column by Michele Landsberg in *Toronto Star*, 1990)

3 / Streep was citing a report issued by the National Commission on Working Women of Wider Opportunities for Women and Women in Film; written by Sally Steenland and titled, "What's Wrong with This Picture? The Status of Women on Screen and behind the Camera in Entertainment TV," and issued in November 1990

4 / National Council of Welfare 1990

5 / *Royal Commission on the Status of Women in Canada* (Ottawa 1970), 14-15

6 / Canadian Radio-television and Telecommunications Commission, *The Portrayal of Gender in Canadian Broadcasting: Summary Report, 1984-1988* (Ottawa: Supply and Services December 1990)

7 / R.S. Abella, *Royal Commission on Equality in Employment* (Ottawa: Supply and Services, October 1984)

8 / City of Toronto, "Progress Report: Equal Opportunity, Goals and Timetables, July 1989-July 1991," Prepared by the Management Services Department and cited in *Toronto Star*, 12 September 1990

9 / Stated by commissioner Adrian Barnes at the Trade Forum held in September 1990 at Toronto's Festival of Festivals.

10 / Research study by Mahoney and Martin for the Caplan-Sauvageau Task Force on Broadcasting Policy (Ottawa 1986)

11 / Ontario Film Development Corporation, "Film and Video Industry Among the Top 20 in the Province but Study Details Serious Concerns for the Future," Press release, 10 July 1990

5 Finetuning the Picture

DEALING WITH THE DATA:
JUST THE FACTS, MA'AM

Data contained in *A Statistical Profile of Women in the Canadian Film and Television Industry* and in other public documents indicate that in 1987/88, the levels of direct public investment in Canadian films and television programs were over $139 million (see table 1). All the government bodies listed in table 1 are financed either at federal or provincial levels to provide investment funding for or generate production/distribution of Canadian programming.

But the level of public investment is much greater than this $139 million figure would imply. A more accurate measure would include each agency's operating or administrative, costs which are also borne by the taxpayer. In addition, it would factor in the 1987/88 programming budgets of such institutions as the English and French television networks of the Canadian Broadcasting Corporation, TV Ontario, and TVO's La Chaine française, Radio-Québec, ACCESS Alberta, and British Columbia's Knowledge Network. These institutions finance the cost of programs generated in-house by staff or contract production teams and, in the case of public television networks, must cover licence fees paid for broadcast rights to programs produced in the independent production sector, both in Canada and abroad.

The amount of public involvement and investment in Canadian film and television is significant on two counts. First, it demonstrates the extent to which such activity relies on public funding; second, it identifies a practical form of leverage which could be developed to resolve the gender imbalance issue. It is improbable that many feature films or indigenous television series would exist without access to the financing found in the deep pockets of Canadian taxpayers, but the relationship between those involuntary investors and the industry they are supporting can be complicated.

With respect to the public sector, tax-generated dollars provide most of the annual operating and production funds for provincial broadcasters, CBC Radio,

TABLE 1
Direct Public Investment

Telefilm Canada	$ 94,791,922
National Film Board	28,546,718
SOGIC	7,011,335
OFDC	3,451,683
Manitoba Culture	307,960
Alberta Development Fund	617,061
BC Film	662,411
Canada Council	1,321,735 (86/87)
Ontario Arts Council	555,689
Total	**$ 139,418,697**

Source: *A Statistical Profile of Women in the Canadian Film and Television Industry,*
Project Report prepared by Peat Marwick Stevenson & Kellogg (Toronto: Toronto
Women in Film and Video 1990)

and the National Film Board. The television services of the CBC and Radio-Canada supplement their portion of parliamentary appropriations with advertising revenue, but pressure is mounting to discontinue this practice.

Production costs for Canadian programs carried by the public networks are either wholly underwritten by a station or network (for example, local news/current affairs, national news, children's series) or licensed for broadcast. In the latter case, a licence fee is negotiated with a private producer who may use the commitment to broadcast as an essential prerequisite in acquiring Telefilm Canada or other agency investment. Occasionally, the network may become a co-producer, making available some of its own production resources in addition to payment of a licence fee. In the case of independent productions, the private producer takes the project proposal and broadcast letter to one or more of the funding agencies which assess script, production plans, and financing to determine the level of public investment. What is clear is that a significant amount of public funding is involved for *all* programs broadcast on public stations and networks.

In the case of private stations and networks, many domestically produced drama series, television movies, as well as some variety, children's and documentary production, are made with the support of Telefilm Canada. In fact, equal proportions of Telefilm's broadcast funding are currently utilized by the national public services and Canada's private commercial broadcasters.

Here again, the prospective producer brings a proposal to a station or network, which negotiates a licence fee and assesses its own additional investment, if any. At the next stage, Telefilm determines its involvement in script and development financing and in production funding which, at least in theory and frequently in practice, could amount to 49 per cent of projected production cost. The remainder of the necessary financing is then acquired through a combination of provincial agency investment, pre-sale, or licence fees from other Canadian or foreign services, private investment, and loans.

In the film sector, public involvement occurs primarily through Telefilm's feature film fund and through the National Film Board of Canada. Although the latter undertakes some co-production of features with the private sector (generally through provision of facilities or other resources), in other production areas most NFB films are completely underwritten from public sources. Less obvious, perhaps, are the funds injected into the film sector by the Sponsored Program Group of Supply and Services Canada, whose non-theatrical production fund amounted to some $1.8 million in each of the last two years. This scheme is designed to assist independent producers in all regions of Canada with development, production, and distribution of film or videotape products intended for educational institutions, libraries, social agencies, industrial or other traditional non-theatrical markets.

Additional federal financial involvement is generated by contracts for advertisement of government programs through television commercials each year. These contracts are administered by designated advertising agencies, who frequently subcontract the actual "shoot" to an independent production house.

While the production environment described above is almost byzantine in its ownership and financial structures, the one constant is a strong public presence in financing, both directly (as investment through Telefilm) and indirectly through payment of licence fees by public broadcasters, sponsorship by the federal government or underwriting the cost of various public agencies which regulate, support, or facilitate the distribution of Canadian television and films (for example, the CRTC, federal and provincial ministries responsible for communications and/or culture, the CBC, Telefilm).

Each and every Canadian taxpayer is a shareholder in the CBC and the NFB, and in all the independently produced television programs and films in which Telefilm is involved. This Telefilm funding is project based and meets criteria established by the funding agency itself. Nevertheless, it results in a strong minority public presence in most independently produced dramatic and variety programming. And these shareholdings are increased by provincial government support initiatives, such as educational broadcasters and production funding agencies.

It would seem reasonable, therefore, that participation of women in these publicly funded activities should at least mirror the demographic representation of women in Canadian society. However, such is not the case.

Data contained in the *Statistical Profile* indicate that 65 per cent of those working in the film and television industry in Canada are male, only 35 per cent are female.[1] (The *Profile* provides statistics on gender participation in three segments of the production industry: production, distribution, and broadcast; figures for the exhibition sector were not available.) The greatest imbalance occurs in the production segment, where the private sector's workforce is only 27 per cent female; in the public sector, women constitute 52 per cent of the labour force. In the broadcast segment, there is no sectoral distinction: both private and public sectors employ only 36 per cent women compared with 64 per cent men. Across the industry, the imbalance would be even more startling were it not for the significant *overrepresentation* of women in the private sector element of distribution (65 per cent).

We are overly familiar with the argument that change in industrial employment patterns takes time, but this contention cannot be held to apply to the political appointments which staff the commissions and boards of directors that supervise and shape the policies of our major public institutions. One might expect, therefore, that this would be the first level at which commitment to gender equity would be reflected. But has it been?

Table 2 provides a breakdown of participation during the past decade and a half on four public sector boards and commissions, those which have the most significance for the development of film and television in this country. During the past 17 years, the participation of women on these boards or commissions which regulate or supervise operations totalling in the billions of dollars of funding, most of it from public sources, has averaged 22 per cent for the Canadian Radio-television and Telecommunications Commission, 19.5 per cent for the CBC, 25 per cent for Telefilm Canada, and 25 per cent for the National Film Board. Clearly, this is not an equitable representation of women by any standard, be the comparison based on population figures (52 per cent female), workforce statistics (43 per cent female), or taxation data (43 per cent of taxable returns filed by females).

Only at Telefilm Canada and at the NFB, the two institutions with a smallest boards, has a reasonable representation of women been achieved, and, in recent years, the presence of a female film commissioner on three of the four governing bodies may be considered a skew factor. Yet this was and is the easiest kind of balance to achieve. No special industrial or other technical expertise has historically been a prerequisite for these political plums and the availability of politically qualified women is not in doubt. Only a lack of real commitment to the gender issue can explain such obvious failure by the federal government to address the question of balance at board levels.

TABLE 2
Representation of Women on Relevant
Federal Boards and Commissions

YEAR	CRTC			CBC/R-C			CFDC TELEFILM			NFB/ONF		
	Posts	#F	%F	Posts†	#F	%F	Posts†	#F	%F	Posts†	#F	%F
1974/75	15	2	8	15	3	20	7	3	43	9	1	11
1975/76	15	2	8	15	3	20	7	2	29	9	1	11
1976/77	19	3	16	15	3	20	7	1	14	9	1	11
1977/78	19	4	21	15	3	20	7	1	14	9	1	11
1978/79	19	5	26	15	2	13	7	1	14	9	1	11
1979/80	19	4	21	15	-	0	7	1	14	9	1	11
1980/81	19	4	21	15	-	0	7	-	0	9	1	11
1981/82	19	4	21	15	-	0	7	-	0	9	2	22
1982/83	19	4	21	15	-	0	7	1	14	9	2	22
1983/84	19	4	21	15	2	13	7	2	29	9	2	22
1984/85	19	4	21	15	4	27	7	2	29	9	2	22
1985/86	19	4	21	15	5	33	7	2	29	9	3	33
1986/87	19	4	21	15	5	33	7	2	29	9	3	33
1987/88	19	6	32	15	5	33	7	3	43	9	5	55
1988/89	19	6	32	15	6	40	7	3	43	9	5	55
1989/90	19	6	32	15	5	33	7	3	43	9	5	55
1990/91	19	5	26	15	4	27	7	3	43	9	3	3

* Includes full and part-time members
† Includes government film commissioner

Small wonder, then, that the private sector has been slow to respond. In private radio and television broadcasting operations,women account for only 1 per cent of senior management and 16 per cent of middle management, while their representation in professional and semi-professional categories is somewhat better, 25 and 22 per cent, respectively. Comparable figures for the public broadcasting sector are slightly more encouraging, with 14 per cent of senior and 19 per cent of middle management identified as female, as are 34 per cent and 27 per cent of those in professional and semi-professional job categories.

Finally, in the independent production sector, figures for 1988 found in the *Statistical Profile* indicates that only 18 per cent of key creative jobs on certified Canadian productions were held by women, with an average of 14 per cent female personnel for all employment categories. There can be no claim that women are "not available" to take jobs in the industry. The same source indicates that of professional screenwriters available, 38 per cent were female but only 17 per cent were employed.

And body counts alone fail to tell the whole story. In general, women are still clustered in secretarial and administrative support functions throughout the industry. They are most significantly underrepresented in the more highly paid senior creative, technical, and management functions, so their share of income generated is proportionately low. It is noteworthy as well that, even in the public sector where a more significant female presence exists in senior management ranks, women are likely to be present in a "term" or temporary capacity, rather than as part of the regular staff complement.

The unavoidable and profoundly disturbing conclusion to be drawn from the figures quoted above and others found in the *Statistical Profile* is that women are not participating equitably in the industry. At a cumulative level, gender imbalance is marked; equally alarming is the fact that many of the women who manage to find employment do so at much less than an optimal level. In these situations, their opportunity to utilize and develop skills and talents is restricted, as is the opportunity for credit and advancement. Is there a remedy?

THE STATUS QUO IN GOVERNMENT: PLUS ÇA CHANGE ...

The Federal Government
Since 1986, the federal government has had in place a policy of employment equity, administered by the Ministry of Employment and Immigration. Section 2 of the Employment Equity Act states that the objective is

to achieve equality in the workplace so that no person shall be denied employment opportunities or benefits for reasons unrelated to ability and ... to correct the conditions of disadvantage in employment experienced by women, aboriginal peoples, persons with disabilities and persons who are, because of their race or colour, in a visible minority in Canada ....

As a result of this legislation, the government has introduced three linked programs:

1 / The Legislated Employment Equity Program requires that all employers with 100 employees or more and who are subject to the Canada Labour Code must implement employment equity, develop specific plans for its achievement, and report annually on their results.

2 / Treasury Board policies require that federal crown corporations and government departments must themselves meet these same requirements; those federal agencies with fewer than 100 employees are required to report annually on the representation of designated groups in their workforce, and to develop action plans that the board will monitor.

3 / The Federal Contractors Program has been instituted to ensure that companies seeking to do business with the federal government also comply with the Employment Equity Program.

It should be noted, however, that this "contract compliance" is applicable only to those companies employing more than 99 persons who are bidding on contracts valued at $200,000 or more. All prospective contractors are required to file with Employment and Immigration Canada (CEIC) an employment equity work plan which identifies the current status of designated employee groups, outlines plans to correct underrepresentation, and sets out a timetable for implementation. Once this submission has been approved, the contractor is required to monitor the workplace and report on progress at least once. Two years after the initial approval, the company becomes eligible for random review, at which point continued improvement in performance respecting the representation of women, the disabled, visible minorities, and native peoples is expected.

One or other of the three initiatives in the Employment Equity Program applies to federal government departments and many of its agencies and, thus, to the Department of Communications, CRTC, CBC, Canada Council, Department of the Secretary of State, and all television licensees which fall under the jurisdiction of the CRTC and have more than 99 employees. The only notable exceptions are provincial educational television stations or networks that are subject to provincial regulation, and the National Film Board, which has developed its own employment equity policy based on section 15 of the Human Rights Act.

In effect, most Canadian film and broadcasting companies are exempt from CEIC's employment equity program because of its high staff threshold level. These corporate entities are, for the most part, relatively small, often short-lived and incorporated for purposes of a single production or series. Staffing is done on a contract basis to meet project-specific needs. In 1987/88, Statistics Canada reported that 520 independent production companies were operational. Only a handful of these – the larger animation houses and vertically integrated production/distribution undertakings – would have been of a size to be affected by employment equity programs. The same is true of most private sector radio and television stations where a permanent staff of 100 would be exceptional.

Even if the threshold trigger-number were lower, it is doubtful the impact would be significant – witness the sluggish rate of progress towards gender balance at such eligible institutions as the CBC and CTV networks. The policy seems to have stopped with the definition of desired corporate behaviours, and no appropriate enforcement mechanisms have been developed to deal with those departments, agencies, and crown corporations who do not or will not comply. Even the CRTC, Canada's broadcast regulator, has lacked the authority to involve itself directly in the internal management practices of those broadcasters it supervises. Its strongest weapon is the "expression of concern," which it can record at the time of licence renewal, but this is not a practice which licensees find intimidating.

The CRTC may, under the terms of new broadcast legislation, have limited discretion to concern itself with gender-related issues. Section 3(1)(*d*)(iii) of the new Broadcasting Act states that "the Canadian broadcasting system should through its programming and the employment opportunities arising out of its operations, serve the needs and interests, and reflect the circumstances and aspirations of Canadian men, women and children, including equal rights ..." This clause could be interpreted as permitting the commission to evaluate network and station employment patterns by gender and establish gender balance as an essential element in its regular supervisory function. An instruction from the minister to whom the CRTC reports would clarify the commission's responsibility in this regard.

Provincial Activity

While some film and television activity takes place in every region of Canada, for decades Ontario has been the anglophone production centre. In the last few years, there has been considerable growth in production activity in British Columbia, especially in the production of foreign films and television series. Nevertheless, the preponderance of anglophone Canadian production and Canadian co-ventures remains centred in Ontario, where these activities are eligible for rebates under the Ontario Film Investment Plan (OFIP).

According to the Ontario Film Development Corporation, the amount spent on independent film and television production in Ontario in 1990 amounted to $254.2 million; in British Columbia, the comparable figure was $188.5 million. A breakdown of those amounts indicates the extent to which foreign production activity presently dominates the B.C. industry (see table 3). The dominance of foreign production in British Columbia is significant because provincial employment equity initiatives have considerably greater impact on companies operating under provincial jurisdiction. Their effect on foreign companies that select a Canadian location and, hence, on Canadians they may contract for services are likely to be minimal.

The policy initiatives of the government of Ontario are of particular interest. More production companies are centred there than in other regions. In 1987/88,

TABLE 3
Domestic and Foreign Production in Ontario and B.C.

1990 Production	British Columbia	Ontario
	(C$ million)	
Canadian and co-ventures	54.3	198
Foreign	134.2	56.2
VALUE OF TOTAL PRODUCTION	188.5	254.2

there were 250 companies active in Ontario, 161 in Quebec, and 209 elsewhere in Canada. Similarly, the principal anglophone television networks, film distribution companies, and cinema chains have headquarters in Ontario and, therefore, its employment policies and legislation are more likely to establish precedents that may be adopted elsewhere.

The Policy of Ontario

At present, Ontario's employment equity policies rest on the Ontario Human Rights Code, which provides for freedom from discrimination in such areas as employment, contracts, and provision of services, and governs provincial ministries and agencies as well as non-governmental employers of any size. Ontario's Employment Standards Act sets minimum standards for the labour force, as well as requiring equal pay for equal work; it applies to all Ontario employers, including production companies which make films and television programs. As noted above, broadcasters themselves fall under federal legislation, the Canada Labour Code.

For several years the Working Group on Employment Equity of the Ontario Ministry of Citizenship has been designing specific equity proposals for Ontario, and several options were presented to cabinet prior to Ontario's election in September 1990. The New Democratic Party government of Premier Bob Rae is committed to the legislation of employment equity. Planning and design of an appropriate process, including implementation and enforcement, are now underway, and introduction of new legislation is expected sometime in 1991. When draft legislation is introduced, it will be the responsibility of women active in Ontario's production industry to ensure that their interests are well served.

The run-up to the provincial election expected in British Columbia in 1991 should also be carefully monitored, and the broad question of gender balance should be made an issue. In the event that the Social Credit government loses power to the NDP, legislative proposals already researched in Ontario may be of interest as the basis of a west coast initiative.

The Province of Quebec

An equity program is also in place in Quebec, where it applies to companies tendering for contracts and to those applying for government subsidy. Here, the triggering numbers are contracts or subsidies of $100,000 or greater, with staff complements of 100 persons or more. Of particular concern is the Société de développement des industries culturelles du Québec (SOGIC), the provincial film and television funding agency, where little or no effort has been made to encourage any form of gender balance at the board or management levels, or in its granting function.

Employment equity and the issue of gender balance have not been a priority in production sectors in Quebec. Only the NFB has made substantial progress, and the other production sectors would do well to borrow from its experience.

Telefilm Canada

Telefilm Canada is an essential funder of both films and television programs. It is used regularly by producers of programs for both private and public television stations and by producers of feature and documentary films. To determine an applicant's eligibility, Telefilm must assess the creative and business viability of each proposal. This evaluation process is detailed, as it should be when dispersal of public funds is at issue. At present, Telefilm has no responsibility for assessing gender balance within personnel contracted for productions it funds, but it would not be implausible for reporting on gender balance of production company and crew to be added to the existing application for Telefilm funding. Such action would permit the tools of contract compliance – already an established element of the equity process – to be modified for application in the film and television production industries.

Telefilm should be required to specify acceptable minimums for gender participation and distribution of earnings within those production companies in whose films or television programs it invests, with gradual increases each year until balance is achieved in the target year of 1999/2000. If action were taken immediately, the policy could be in place by fiscal year 1992/93, allowing eight years of gradual development, a pace which would impose no untoward disruption on the production community. Of equal importance, this time frame would allow women in the production sector to develop and expand their skills with reasonable expectations that appropriate employment opportunities would appear.

Such action would require no new legislation; a policy decision by the board of Telefilm Canada would be sufficient to launch the process. Nor would such a plan carry the stigma of mandatory government interference in creative decisions. No producer would be forced to participate; only those independent production companies wishing to make use of public funds to partially underwrite their production activity would be subject to compliance assessment.

CONTRACT COMPLIANCE:
TAKING THE NEXT STEP

The federal government's approach to contract compliance has only limited application to film and television production, but there are other models that are potentially more appropriate. One of the most sophisticated is that introduced in 1989 by the City of Toronto.

The Toronto Model

Toronto's Task Force on Contract Compliance recommended that public funds should be used to achieve equal opportunity, especially among disadvantaged categories of women, minorities, and people with disabilities. The task force researched the representation of target groups in the city's labour force, among board and commission employees, and in various city-supported public agencies. Companies bidding on contracts and supplied goods/services to the city were also surveyed. These statistics provided a base-line against which future changes in employment and earnings patterns could be assessed.

The public sector portion of the contract compliance program was the first to be introduced; then, in July 1989, the program was extended to the private sector, to cover "all goods and services purchased externally by the City." *All* companies doing business with the city are required to file equal opportunity forms providing data on sex, race, disability status, occupation, and earnings for both their permanent and temporary workers. The data are confidential and are used as the base-line audit. An up-date of these forms will be required in July 1991. Smaller firms (under 50 employees) have the option to use simplified forms.

The city takes the view that employment equity must be a universal principle: there is no allowance for "special cases" or exemptions. Analysis of its impact in the first two quarters of operation indicates that 85 per cent of Toronto's contract dollars are being spent with firms participating in and committed to the equal opportunity program. Toronto, along with the governments of Canada and Quebec, is the only jurisdiction that has begun to use contract compliance as a tool for enforcement of employment equity. Toronto's program is by far the most comprehensive and appears to have had the greatest impact.

Prior to the 1990 election, the government of Ontario was unable to adopt Toronto's approach – in part because of the province's decentralized purchasing policy, with each department and regional office acquiring its own goods and services. There was no mechanism by which the necessary research and monitoring of contract compliance could be efficiently introduced. Changes in that process may, however, be introduced, and the province's employment equity program, to be announced in the fall of 1991, may contain stringent contract compliance mechanisms.

Potential Pitfalls

As with any government program, the efficacy and impact of the contract compliance mechanism are directly related to (a) the accuracy of information on which it is based; (b) categories and definitions appropriate to target industries; (c) comprehensiveness of the program; and (d) appropriate sanctions for demonstrated non-compliance. With careful planning and design, it is possible to avoid the pitfalls.

Canada is in the early days of employment equity, and efforts, though well intentioned and sincere, have generally been limited. An exception to that norm was the autumn 1989 decision by the Ontario College of Art to hire only qualified female candidates to fill teaching vacancies that occur as a result of staff retirements until such time as gender balance of the faculty is achieved.

Gender balance in both the decision-making and creative components of Canada's media is of particular importance to the making of our myths and messages, to the shaping of our society, and the choices we make about our collective future. The images presented by the electronic media are critical to these processes. At a time when we are engaged in serious efforts to reconfigure our national, economic and political structures, it is particularly important that action be taken to ensure balanced gender representation in television and film. At a time when most jurisdictions and many industries are addressing the same fair-employment issues, there can be no justification for exempting Canada's film and television industries.

A Model for Practical Change

Whatever process is introduced must be both simple to administer *and* effective in achieving the eventual objective of gender balance across various job categories within the television and film production sector. Personnel must be experienced and knowledgeable, and crew members cannot be hired simply on the basis of sex. Job opportunities should also be available in all aspects of production so that women can acquire the necessary and progressive experience. For this reason we suggest that this effort to generate employment equity in publicly funded independent television and film should be based on annual incremental increases in:

• the overall participation rate by females in each applicant company's staff and contract complement; and

- the percentage of production-related earnings, exclusive of deferrals and payments to performers, received by female production personnel.

CONCLUSION

This is a practical proposal. It expands the opportunities for the employment of women in all sectors and segments of Canada's film and television community. Yet no major disruptions to existing creative or management processes are imposed. No huge new reporting or administrative burdens are involved, only a modest amount of routine review by Telefilm bureaucrats already accustomed to monitoring productions as agents for the Canadian public. To complete the picture, responsibility for collection, assembly and reporting of the necessary data is assigned.

There is no requirement for new legislation. A simple policy decision taken by Telefilm Canada is all that is needed to start the process. With this model in place, similar action by other public agencies (provincial film funding corporations and arts councils, for example) will be encouraged. And in recognition of concerns of the independent production sector, the criterion would not be mandatory; rather it would apply only to productions seeking access to the involuntary funding support of Canadian taxpayers, almost half of whom are women.

What this proposal *does* provide is a gradual and practical move toward equitable representation in today's most influential media. Canada cannot afford to deny half its population a fair opportunity to participate and, with this proposal, we begin the process of refocusing the picture.

NOTES

1 / *A Statistical Profile of Women in the Canadian Film and Television Industry*, Project Report prepared by Peat Marwick Stevenson & Kellogg (Toronto: Toronto Women in Film and Video 1990) is the source of the figures cited here and later.

6 Action/Reaction: Focus on film and video education

The *Statistical Profile of Women in the Canadian Film and Television Industry* identified the number of women who are enroled in, graduating from, and teaching at postsecondary courses in film and television in Canada.''[1] It found that women represent about one-third of students in their final year of film/broadcasting programs, with the largest percentage in Ontario. Because few institutions monitor graduate placement rates according to gender, it does not provide a statistically significant analysis of employment patterns. Finally, based on the schools that responded, 85 per cent of film/broadcasting program faculty are male and 15 per cent are female.

THE NEED FOR TRAINING WOMEN
TO ASSUME CREATIVE ROLES

Joan Pennefather, chair of the National Film Board, recently released a series of objectives and strategic principles for the period 1990-93 that include a renewed commitment to documentary, to women's films, and "to filmmakers who take risks, experiment with new forms and content, propose new perspectives and display courage and imagination when dealing with complex and controversial subjects."[2] Because many women in the industry choose "independent" films and documentaries to express their vision, this policy alone will create a greater opportunity for women filmmakers.

Affirmative action will increase the demand for more education of women as filmmakers. It may also change the character of what is considered to be marketable within the industry. Broadcasting, both news and series production, plus the mainstream of the film industry have for many years been driven by a market need perceived as being the "action" model. News has not been considered news unless there was a perceived conflict. Only recently have the dangers of this emphasis been scrutinized. The CBC, for example, was widely criticized in the summer of 1990 because its coverage of Meech Lake and Oka was seen as exacerbating the conflict rather than reporting it. Similarly, the

North American English language film industry and series television have centred their programming around adventure pictures oriented largely to young men. *Batman, Raiders of the Lost Arc*, and the CBC series "Urban Angel" all fall into this model. Conflict-driven sports such as hockey and football dominate a vast amount of prime-time television. Recent demographic analysis suggests, however, that though there may be short-term gain financially through adventure pictures, they do not address the market of the majority, which includes children, women, and the general population over 55 years of age. The market-driven economy may well be forced into a dramatic shift in focus.

Economist Harry Hillman Chartrand analyses these changes in a 1988 Canada Council study, *The Crafts in the Post-Modern Economy ... the pattern which sells the things*.[3] Chartrand, who characterizes film, television, and recording as falling within the tradition of the craft and artists guilds, notes:

There are three fundamental demographic changes that are contributing to the growth in arts participation and the emergence of the arts as a significant factor of economic production. These are rising levels of education, increasing participation of women and the aging population.

He argues that "women in North America have traditionally been considered the carriers or guardians of culture," and maintains that "the increasing role of women in the economy and politics will, in and of itself, lead to increasing political and economic recognition of arts and culture" and thus will affect the marketplace.

Post-secondary institutions must therefore ensure that women are trained to fill this new market. They must educate more women as writers, directors, producers, editors, cinematographer/videographers, and educators. They should integrate films and videos by women in theory and history classes to submit them to sound critical analysis and to place them in the overall history of the media. They must also provide an environment in which women can thrive.

THE STATE OF THINGS NOW

The 1990 *Film Canada Yearbook* lists twenty-five post-secondary institutions with film and video programs in English and French Canada. They range in length and scope from a two-year diploma to post-graduate studies. Limited time and resources confine my analysis to four schools, chosen for their size, location, programs, and contrasts in handling gender equity: Simon Fraser University in Burnaby, B.C., Ryerson Polytechnical Institute in Toronto, York University in Downsview, Ont., and Concordia University in Montreal. All these programs include writing, directing, editing, cinematography or video-graphy, producing, theory, and history as part of their course of studies, and they have all with varying degrees of success, addressed the need to provide a larger role for women within their programs.

Representatives of each school were asked in interviews whether they had a gender equity plan in place and, if so, how it was being implemented. They were asked to comment on the findings in the *Statistical Profile*, particularly in regard to the education sector, and their programs were compared with the national figures. They were also asked how their courses of study could help train more women in the creative roles of the industry.

HIRING PATTERNS

Simon Fraser and Concordia film production programs are small programs within relatively small Fine Arts Departments. They have a proportionately large number of women as senior faculty and both have gender equity policies in development but not currently in place. Ryerson and York, in contrast, have large film and video departments and, because of their age and entrenched faculties, they have had to establish firm equity policies and guidelines to address the status quo.

A cursory analysis of hiring patterns suggests that faculties have developed in phases. First, specialists, often nearing retirement, were recruited. Second, graduates who had achieved considerable experience in the industry or in postgraduate education outside the country were employed. Third, graduates from American graduate schools and refugees from behind the Iron Curtain were added in the late 1960s, when most of the new film schools bloomed and expanded, and came to dominate the production programs. Tenured faculties, which were overwhelmingly male, became entrenched and, because of spending cuts throughout the university system, did not expand. For more than fifteen years the only positions open to women within the system have been as part-time, long-term temporary, and tenure-track junior positions. Even part-time positions were largely filled by men.

Gender equity hiring policies have established what appear to be special positions for women. Many faculties view these policies as a way of denying qualified men who have held long-term temporary appointments access to tenure. Until the late 1970s few women had graduated from postgraduate film and video production programs. Even fewer had extensive production experi-ence. By 1982, when they were ready and available to assume a leadership role within the university system, a universal freeze was put on hiring. The Ontario university system was particularly hard hit and is currently caught in the dilemma of being the most poorly funded university system in the country and the province with the most progressive employment equity policies.

A QUALITATIVE PROFILE

Concordia University

The three-year course at Concordia University's Department of Cinema in Montreal is the only film production program where the head of production is a woman and the only program where 50 per cent of the full-time permanent faculty are women. One-third of the students are women. Although an equity policy for the Fine Arts Department is currently being developed, the head of film production sees the strong showing of women faculty in her department as the result of an evolutionary process, rather than a conscious policy. In fact, because there is no policy, it can be seen as mirroring the systemic discrimination that results from women hiring their own kind in the same manner that men have traditionally hired their own.

Concordia offers two kinds of production classes. Female students appear to be attracted to and to perform better in courses oriented to individual production, where they work on their own rather than in teams. As in many other schools, women generally retreat from camera work by third year.

York University

Because of recent Ontario employment equity guidelines and a lower retention rate for women in its programs, York University has developed a gender equity policy and an affirmative action plan specific to the Department of Film & Video. The affirmative action plan recognizes that women bring to "their creative endeavours in film and video valuable perspectives, sensibilities and habits unshared, for the most part, by men," and, therefore, that film and video schools must include tenured women professors capable of sharing their knowledge with all the students, and, in particular, of serving as role models for the women among them.[4] Two out of six tenure-track appointments made in the last ten years at York have been made to women, and half the part-time appointments in production have been filled by women. In 1990-91 women account for 17 per cent of the faculty complement, approximately 28 per cent of the undergraduate students, and 35 per cent of the graduate students. By 1992 the ratio of female to male faculty should reach 30 per cent. As in most production schools, however, teachers need to have a strong generalist production knowledge. Although it has been possible to find two women qualified to teach production within the tenure stream, "it is extremely unlikely that the potential pool of qualified women filmmakers with high levels of technical training will significantly increase ... in the near future: hence, *it is extremely unlikely that we shall soon be able to count on a sizable number of qualified women applicants for studio positions in film and video, regardless of our recruiting efforts.*"[5] The affirmative action plan suggests that, to meet gender equity goals, positions should be created in writing and studies (history and theory) where there is a larger talent pool of women candidates.

The Affirmative Action Plan and
Problems of Implementation

York University is concerned that although it has been successful in filling two production positions with women candidates, earlier appointments, filled by similarly qualified men, were at a higher rank. The designation of positions as assistant professor rather than associate professor, is the result of deteriorating economic conditions within the university system. It would appear that affirmative action guidelines are being filled through the hiring of two women for the price of one man. This clearly jeopardizes the positive intent of pay equity and ensures that women not only remain on the bottom of the pay scale throughout their tenure, but, because they are the same age as their male colleagues, retire with significantly lower pensions.

The university is also re-evaluating the curriculum to ascertain why there is a lower retention rate for women students than for men. It is not unusual for there to be only one woman in the final year and, overall, the percentage of women entering the program has declined. One possible explanation is that the choice of films made in fourth year has historically been based on the perceived ''market.'' The current market is for action pictures made for television. According to a number of faculty, because of the structure of the course and film funding, scripts that are expressed through a woman student's voice are not eligible for production unless they conform to the action-picture model. Women are not given a chance to assume the creative roles in a film unless they imitate their male colleagues. Ways must be found to encourage male and female producers to produce stories by women and men, directed by women and men, shot by women and men, edited by women and men, and of interest to women and men. The institutionalisation of the action picture as the standard at university is detrimental to the development of films about anything else besides other films. The graduate program at York is much more flexible than the undergraduate program. It admits more women to the program and is cognizant of its responsibility to educate future educators. In order to fill the demand for more women professors, graduate schools have a responsibility to recruit more production students and to make their programs more attractive to women.

Ryerson Polytechnical Institute

Ryerson Polytechnical Institute has three schools (School of Radio and Television Arts, Film and Photography Department, School of Journalism) and four programs that involve writing, producing, directing, camera, and editing for film and video. It is by far the largest communications school in the country and one of the largest on the continent. Ryerson has a much lauded gender equity policy that has been in place since 1984. Ryerson's employment equity advisory committee has formulated recommendations and strategies for increasing the proportion of full-time female faculty in departments where they are underrepresented. Although overall equity goals were set for departments, the implementation plans are developed by individual departments on a case-by-case basis. The plan, approved by the Ontario Human Rights Commission in January 1989, "indicates that 57 (out of approximately 72) position(s) vacated by faculty retirements over the next ten years should be designated "equity positions."[6]

The success of the gender equity policy has varied wildly, depending on the willingness of the departments to buy onto it, the age of the faculty, and the administration's readiness to support its own goals. For example, the majority of women hired at Ryerson in the last ten years are part-time and sessional members of the Canadian Union of Education Workers (CUEW). Ryerson's equity policy does not apply to these positions. The policy to fill retired tenured positions with women was suspended because of budget constraints, and the number of part-time positions has been cut radically (from 150 to 90) with more cuts are to follow. In fall 1990, in exchange for six Ryerson Faculty Association tenured positions and 11 limited-term contracts (LTF) to be awarded on seniority, CUEW bargained away "priority of consideration status," that is, job security for most of its members. Few women, if any, had the seniority to qualify for the designated tenure or LTF contracts. Even though there is employment equity at Ryerson, there are fewer opportunities for women this year than last.

The Film and Photography Department comprises three programs: Still Photography, Film Studies, and Media Arts. Since its establishment in the late 1940s as a photography school, photographers have dominated the faculty. Although the film and media arts programs have grown enormously, the tenured faculty remains small and a large percentage of the teaching is by part-time faculty. Currently, only two out of 26 tenured positions (7.6 per cent) are held by women, none of them in production. Although when the revised programs were implemented five years ago there was an unwritten policy to recruit more female faculty and students, that commitment has not been sustained. The percentage of course hours taught by women in the film program has declined from 11 per cent in 1988-90 to 4 per cent in 1990-91. And there are no women among the CUEW faculty eligible for transfer to tenure stream and long-term temporary faculty. The department does not have an affirmative action plan and the chair feels that, given external conditions, his hands are tied. The curriculum of both these programs encourages students to learn all aspects of production. Students have the choice of working in crews or independently. Many of the women choose to work on small budget personal films for economic as well as aesthetic and social reasons.

This lack of concern about maintaining gender balance has extended to enrolment. Student enrolment patterns indicate that in 1991 the number of female students, both applying and accepted, has dropped in both film and media arts programs. Although in fourth-year film 45 per cent of the students in 1990-91 are women, and in media arts 58 per cent are women, there is a drop in first year to 20 per cent in film and 34 per cent in media arts. Given the overall drop in women's participation in the department, these figures suggest that, to attract eligible women, there is a need for firm, written, recruiting policies and an implementation plan that is enthusiastically endorsed by faculty and administration alike.

In contrast, the School of Radio and Television Arts (RTA) and the broadcasting major in Journalism have both implemented gender equity policies. These schools are training the on- and off-camera crews of the major networks in large numbers and their graduates, as producers, anchors, station managers, writers, directors, electronic camera operators, and editors, have come to dominate news and series production in Canada. Both programs report that more than 50 per cent of their students are women.

RTA is actively recruiting more women faculty to provide solid role models for the student body, which is now 60 per cent women. The chair has suggested that, in screening applicants for personal drive, commitment, ability to finish, evidence of mixing with society, and interest in new information rather than hardware, women have recently outperformed men in entering this very competitive program.

Recruiting new faculty has not been as easy, since women's career paths are different from men's. Because of their child-rearing responsibilities, women tend to concentrate on specific areas of expertise, while men acquire wider experience. All production schools need professors who can teach a wide range of courses and, unfortunately, not many women match in career breadth their male counterparts. The strategy in RTA has been to hire women first as part-timers, in order to employ them full time in the future. How this is going to be accomplished, given the recent cut backs within the part-time faculty remains to be seen. Nevertheless, RTA has one women among four full-time faculty, and seven women among 19 part-timers who teach production.

Women have traditionally shied away from technology, and it has been suggested that only 20 per cent of the courses in technology are attractive to women. Yet in RTA like elsewhere women tend to become independent producers, where they have to do everything. The RTA faculty is currently re-evaluating the way technology is taught to ensure that all students are thoroughly familiar and comfortable with the materials, techniques, and principles that underline the mechanics of production.

The school that has made the most progress towards gender equity is the School of Journalism, where most of the few professional female camera operators in Canada received their training. Women have formed 60 per cent of the student body for the last six years, mainly because in journalism there are visible role models for women. The School of Journalism takes the position that, although women have not filled large-scale management roles in print and broadcasting, women are no less ambitious than men. Indeed, because they are more collaborative, women make good managers. Here, women are being encouraged to "break the glass ceiling" between the newsroom and management.

The School of Journalism has recently appointed three women to the tenure stream, meaning women now fill six of the 14 positions. The chair attributes the success of the gender equity program to the fact that the faculty set goals and refused to give them up without a fight. Following the principle that it is critical the media reflect society, the School of Journalism is embarking on a more extensive equity program that will include all members of society hitherto denied access because of race, sex, or physical disability.

Simon Fraser University

The film program at Simon Fraser University forms a small part of the Fine Arts Department. Currently, there is no formal equity policy in regard to admissions or hiring. Of the students, 40 per cent are women and of the faculty, 25 per cent are women; as senior professors, they outrank their male colleagues. The strength and renown of the female faculty has created an environment where the students can exhibit independence and commitment. The devotion of this department to independent filmmaking has attracted a strong group of filmmakers, both male and female, who are committed to ideas. They have addressed the insecurity many women feel towards technology and particularly lighting (most women, and some men, know little about electricity) by providing special tutorials on technology, for those without the necessary background.

Films made by women, and particularly women graduates of the program, are shown at subsidised screenings, often under the auspices of external agencies that deal with women's roles in society. The Vancouver film collective, Women in Focus, has also provided a powerful model and resource. Many of the Simon Fraser students get their first credits while working as informal apprentices on films produced by members of Women in Focus. Another organization, Vancouver Women in Film and Video, initiated a series of sessions on "producing for women." The workbook produced in this experiment has been used throughout the country. Similar sessions, perhaps in conjunction with existing film production programs, should be held in all major filmmaking regions.

THE EFFECT OF MARGINALIZATION OF
WOMEN WITHIN THE SCHOOLS

The murder of 14 female engineering students in Montreal in December 1990 made it essential for all post-secondary institutions where women are educated in "non-traditional" roles to examine their complicity in fostering negative attitudes towards women. Since the media is one of the main subliminal forces in the institutionalization of violence against women in our society, it is imperative, if we wish as a society to prevent the marginalization and brutalization of women, that women perform roles in the media that reflect their numbers.

The schools are the ground where the ideas of the media makers are cultivated. We can no longer afford to entrench the action picture as the norm. The boys' club atmosphere that has dominated production faculties must be re-examined in light of its negative impact on the way we portray ourselves as a society. Subjects by women, which have tended to centre around family (*Bye Bye Blues*), values (*Not a Love Story* or *If You Love This Planet*) or personal vision (*My Marilyn*), although exhibited widely at film festivals, have tended to be classified as art films that are self-consciously earnest, too controversial, or too personal for wide public distribution. Not only do we have to create a vehicle for women's voices to be heard, but we have to accept that men need women as positive role models and mentors as much as women.

Women with few exceptions form a minority in film and broadcasting schools. This marginalisation of women faculty and students sets them apart from the perceived norm and, as a result, many complain that far too much attention is focused on them as individuals. A number of women shared the experience of being directly attacked and verbally abused by students and faculty who would not have approached a male faculty member in the same way.

Physical Harassment

"There is a terrible problem with male students and anything that reeks of feminism ..." "With female students, they get destroyed unless they are very strong or have strongly supportive male or female profs"

"Female faculty have been crucified by young men who lash out"

Two young women professors

One instructor, who was covering for an ailing male colleague, was interrupted when a student barged into her class and harassed her about a problem he was having booking equipment. She asked him to leave and he complied, but later, when she encountered him in a hallway, he physically and verbally abused her in front of another faculty member and a student.

One faculty member described the high drop-out rate of women students in terms of peer-group pressure: "There are a certain number of women who come in who know they want to be a producer, writer and directors. Those that come in and get squashed may be ambivalent about what they want to do ... on the other hand, they may not want to be one of the boys."

There doesn't appear to be any recognition of, or administrative process in place, to deal with the ritualized behaviour of adolescents towards women. The perception that it is acceptable to scream and yell, because you can get away with it with Mommy, but with Daddy law and order applies -- has not been addressed as a problem within the education system. It is unfortunate that a number of female faculty reported that their fifty-year-old male colleagues have behaved towards them in a similar way.

Sexual Coercion and Harassment

Inappropriate sexual relations between male faculty and female students have always been endemic in fine arts faculties, though few complaints have been made because both participants are usually willing. There is a feeling among concerned male and female faculty, however, that engaging in these non-professional relationships is an abuse of professional ethics. The relationship between teacher and student is privileged, and in other professions any intimacy would be considered professional misconduct and a breach of trust. Policies must be put in place by boards of governors and faculty associations that outline acceptable relations between women and men in a professional situation, particularly when there is the potential for abuse of power.

The fact that inappropriate relations are so systemically tolerated is detrimental to creating a climate for students to become self-actualized professionals. The systemic exploitation of young female (and sometimes male) students by male faculty is perhaps one of the reasons for the resistance and anger shown by the faculty in fine arts and applied arts schools towards the implementation of gender equity.

A part-time instructor at one university recalled an incident during her first year of teaching. She was evaluated by a senior tenured male faculty member. After having an extended intellectual discussion about school and curriculum, a piece of paper was ripped, a phone number was written down, and she was told, "My wife is away, why don't you call me at home?" She had not seen her evaluation yet and found his response not only inappropriate but threatening. Ten minutes later, fuming, she encountered another male faculty member. "I was wearing a long Mexican pendant and he pulled it and poked it in my breast. There was no one I could talk to at that time. Can you imagine how it would affect a defenceless female student?''

Course evaluations, a device established by departments and student unions to give students input into course quality, are often used as a device for students to get back at their professors. Women faculty expressed concern that students use evaluations to express their discomfort with the difference in gender between them and their professors. This is particularly true for students whose culture doesn't accept women in authority. Programs should be put in place to help students adjust and training should be available to female faculty to help them deal with conflicts that arise from cultural acclimatization problems.

If the schools want to create an environment that is attractive to women faculty and students, rather than threatening, they must answer to a little ''self-conscious earnestness'' and address the systemic problems and misconceptions regarding women and their roles.

NOTES

1 / *A Statistical Profile of Women in the Canadian Film and Television Industry*, Project Report prepared by Peat Marwick Stevenson & Kellogg (Toronto: Toronto Women in Film and Video 1990)

2 / Leo Rice-Barker, "The NFB assesses the state of its art," *Playback*, 29 October 1990

3 / Harry Hillman Chartrand, *The Crafts in the Post-Modern Economy ... the pattern which sells things*, Working Document 6-238 (Ottawa: Canada Council 20 May 1988), 15-16

4 / Department of Film & Video, Faculty of Fine Arts, York University, "Draft Affirmative Action Plan," 1 June 1990

5 / Ibid.

6 / Background Information on the Development of Employment and Educational Equity at Ryerson, November 1989

LOUISE SURPRENANT

7 Employment, Women and the Film and Television Industry in Quebec

CURRENT SITUATION

Agencies and Legislation

For a long time, Quebec has claimed jurisdiction over communications including the film and broadcasting industry. In this article, I will not focus on the specifics of Quebec culture and its various modes of expression, but primarily on the possibilities of integrating women into the film and video industry.

We need to reflect deeply on the situation in order to bring about concrete, political action. Thus we will be able to define the needs of women and determine the obstacles and constraints that prevent them from entering professional fields. In this respect an awareness of various realities in the working world is needed to ensure fair representation of women in the professional workforce.

In Quebec, there is no official information on women's access to the film industry or on their role in this industry. In 1982, the government of Quebec set up the Fournier Commission to study the film and broadcasting. The commission studied the future of film, and state intervention in production, distribution, and operations while keeping in mind two basic objectives: to revitalize and to create dialogue in both the public and private sector of this industry.

Two organizations, the Institut québécois du cinéma (IQC) and the Société de développement des industries culturelles du Québec (SOGIC), have already received a mandate to evaluate policies and to set up assistance programs for companies. A third organization, the Régie du cinéma, was given the task of classification and issuing licences.

With the exception of various recommendations on funding research, the provincial commissions concerned with the development and management of financial resources and policies for the Quebec film industry do not have any data on the situation of women in the film industry and do not consider it a priority issue.

No mention whatsoever was made of equity or equal opportunity. It was only in 1984 that the government of Quebec passed an act respecting equal access programs. Equal access programs may have been a favourable step for salaried female employees working in other industries, however, women who want to benefit from these programs must be working on a "permanent" basis.

The majority of women in the film industry are employed on a contract or freelance basis just like most of their male counterparts. It is therefore impossible for them to demand equal pay or a promotion under the equity act in Quebec.

The government agencies do not have to respect equity except to specify that positions advertised are open to both men and women. That issue is also of no concern to those that receive funds from para-public agencies. SOGIC is not interested in whether a man or woman submits a request for a loan, investment, or support for a film or television production or who the loan is for; it is more interested in the "commercial," and profitable aspects of the production. The organization should at the very least study this aspect by keeping track of the percentage of men and women. We feel this not likely to occur, however, given the fact that all of the project development officers at SOGIC are men. The equity principle is therefore still foreign to the organization that makes decisions about public funding.

Furthermore, men and women producers are not really concerned with this problem. With no great interest and no adequate legislation, they are not under any obligation to encourage or even to allow women greater access to jobs traditionally held by men. It would be false to claim that there aren't enough women available to meet the market needs. The truth is that the figures provided by the Syndicat des techniciennes et des techniciens du cinéma et de la vidéo du Québec (STCVQ) reveal that there are more women than ever before working in almost every sector. However, when we look at key positions and positions of responsibility recognized by the status of the artist act, the difference is noticeable and the division between men and women is no longer equal.

Women appear to have fair representation in all of the sectors. However, when the percentages of men and women working in positions of responsibility or as assistants or support staff are examined, we notice that most heads in the various sectors are in fact men.

In the directory of STCVQ members, executive and creative positions recognized by the act are divided into 16 categories: director of photography, camera operator, manager, still photographer, editor, sound editor, art director, head production designer and production designer, head makeup artist, makeup artist and special effects makeup artist, costume designer, head hairstylist, hairstylist, and scenic painter. The distribution of women and men is given below.

	Director Photo.	Camera Operator	Art Director	Production Designer	Costume Designer	Makeup Artist	Hair-stylist	Editor
M	41	5	9	8	3	1	12	14
F	0	0	2	1	7	0	5	5

It would be false to conclude that most of these positions are held by men because women are simply not interested. Exhibit III-2 of the *Statistical Profile* illustrates very clearly that men hold most positions of responsibility in the private sector.

I took the liberty of looking into key positions, namely those considered as "department" head in certain sectors including direction, and editing, where women hold the majority of positions but have less responsibility. Women are employed as assistants, trainees, and collaborators, often in numbers. Why do women make such excellent, responsible, and disciplined assistants and yet few or no women at all are heads of sectors? Why can't they reach the higher ranks in the industry?

The list of members at the Association québécoise des réalisateurs et réalisatrices de cinéma et de télévision (AQRRCT) enables us to assess the number of women members compared to men members. However, we must not forget that membership is free and not mandatory for people who work in the industry, unlike most other contract trades in the industry. At the end of 1990, women represented only 25 per cent of the association. This is far from the ratio in the film industry.

The questions that arise about this situation are very worrisome. Is the film industry to become or remain a male ghetto that is particularly difficult to get into? Would women only be allowed to make a few occasional films on so-called typical women's subjects?

In 1990, Marquise Lepage, president of the AQRRCT, denounced this situation in a letter supported by the association. Mme Lepage stressed that not one feature film was produced by a woman in 1989. She also underlined the fact that not one woman was in charge of project development at the SOGIC and that access to the position was restricted.

During a meeting on the film school to be opened in Quebec in 1991, the association also recommended that the principle of equity between men and women be enforced: "that equity between men and women be respected at all levels of the project when forming the general assembly and the board of directors, as well as selecting students, professors, and tutors."

It is common knowledge that equal access does not appear in the mandate of the Société let alone in that of the Institut du cinéma québécois. And these organizations play an advisory role to the minister. They formulate recommendations that they feel represent vital aspects of our industry and prepare studies upon the request of the Ministère des Affaires culturelles. To the best of our knowledge, the ministry has not shown any interest in the problem of equity in the film industry and has not requested any studies on the subject.

Canada is also searching for a consensus on the main issues in professional training in the cultural sector. We are therefore at the stage of development where we can demand a free curriculum which encompasses who we are and what we want to become:

The Study Group will be particularly concerned with the situation of women in professional arts training.

In spite of the progress made, recent studies confirm that stereotypes still exist as well as unequal pay and lack of access to certain positions and trades. These factors, among many others, discourage women from learning these trades.

Throughout the meeting, there was a constant effort to feminize terms and to encourage individual assistance programs and the relationship between professional training and work in the industry. This leads us to believe that the study group will be addressing the access of women in film to training programs. Once again, this step will not apply to all of Quebec because education falls under provincial jurisdiction. Nevertheless, we could make note of opinions and recommendations in order to put pressure on regional authorities.

In practice, equal access to SOGIC programs will only be possible when there is formal support for it. The advisors to the Ministère des Affaires culturelles could make this recommendation to the ministry and all matters concerning film, video, and television would benefit from equal access, whether it be to programs organized by SOGIC or the Ministère des Affaires culturelles to assist production and research, outside of the activities of its civil servants.

There is a need for adequate training to permit access for women to non-traditional industry occupations. When the Canadian and Quebec film industry first began, on-the-job training was the norm. However, there is now an overspecialization, which suggests that training better suited to the needs of the industry is required.

The decision was made in Quebec to create the Institut national de l'image et du son (INIS). This new institution is supposed to respond to a widely expressed need in the industry. In 1990, the Institut québécois held talks with the various professional associations in order to finalize this project. Some associations, such as the AQRRTF, stressed the need for equity in all sectors affected by this institution.

On a different note, the National Federation of Communication Workers received a mandate to form a status of women committee which would look into work sectors, schedules, operations and working conditions, etc. Its report, entitled "L'Urgence d'agir" presents the results of a questionnaire completed by the various unions of the National Federation of Communication Workers.

The results revealed that most regular part-time jobs are held by women (78.2 per cent). The ratio of men to women in jobs covered by a collective agreement was also revealed:

Communications (research, host): 1 woman to 2.5 men
Service (reception, sales, distribution): where the trends are most equal, 1.8 per cent in favour of women
Office (administration): largely dominated by women, 1 man to 5 women
Trade (maintenance, repairs): predominantly male.

Women therefore represent a majority in the office and service sectors, but men represent a majority in all others. It is important to note that these sectors are the least well paid and the most vulnerable to cuts because of factors such as technological advances. Almost 75 per cent of the part-time jobs are held by women. While it is true that women sometimes request part-time work, the fact is that it is almost impossible for these women to find full-time employment.

Another important point in this study is the reference to employer discrimination against women (discrimination is explained as encompassing looks, gestures, behaviour, attitudes, actions, or policies where women are treated differently than men). This is a topic that is rarely discussed by women and the results of a confidential study reveal only the tip of the iceberg.

The following types of discrimination were noted:

Access to promotion 64.3%	Intense supervision 28.6%
Disregard of opinions 42.9%	Working conditions 21.4%
Paternalistic behaviour 42.9%	Language 21.4%
Maternity-child care 35.7	Sexual harassment 21.4%
Age 35.7%	Salary 21.4%
Physical appearance 35.6%	Subservience (serve coffee) 14.3%

THE STATE IN 1990

In a working paper prepared for talks with film organizations and associations in June 1990, the Ministère des Affaires culturelles of Quebec presented an overview of the problems in the Quebec film industry. This document identified the industry's strengths and weaknesses and said "We can only provide solutions and make changes after the situation has been studied in great depth."

The working paper makes a lot of references to investment, tax measures, and research and development, but the important point is what results from this analysis – an administrative procedure that does not favour creativity and unresolved difficulties in training and professional development for film professionals. The paper does not make any mention whatsoever of equity, equal opportunity, positive reinforcement, women's access to film production, distribution, operations, training, or education.

In this study of the film industry with a view to future changes to both the organizations and laws that govern the industry, the ministry refers only to traditionally held viewpoints. For example, videography development and access centres subsidized by the Canada Council and artists' centres subsidized by the Ministère des Affaires culturelles have enabled an increasingly large number of women to enter filmmaking through producing a video.

To give an example of this, suffice it to say that during a meeting of the Alliance de la vidéo et du cinéma indépendant held in Halifax in 1989, the majority of video directors and producers were women. This also proves that no matter how small the opportunity, as soon as women find it, they have an increasing and persistent interest in playing their role in the industry. The women who work at centres across Canada represented or directed most of these centres. After film was introduced and the financial means were much greater, the people in charge of production and distribution were all men. This is simply a factual observation without any detailed study, but nevertheless exemplary.

INTERNATIONAL CONFERENCE

In November 1989, women from various countries met in Berlin to define the situation of women in the film and broadcasting industry. These women felt that the battle for equal opportunity was part of the battle for the survival of national production reflecting the respective cultural identities. My report is in keeping with this vision of national culture and its survival.

Documents on equal opportunity and equal pay have been published by the International Labour Office (ILO) outlining equal treatment for women in the working world. The women at the conference based their discussions on these ILO documents.

Some of the women at this conference reported inexplicable situations in their respective countries:

German Democratic Republic	47 per cent of the co-ordinators are women In feature film studios, there are two women for every 30 men
Sweden	15 per cent of television technicians are women 200 professions exclusively for men, 300 men are directors
France	66 per cent of the people making minimum wage are women
Japan	17 per cent women work for the 5 major television stations and 6 per cent work in production
Czechoslovakia	radio and television personnel, 60 per cent women editing directors, 47 per cent women chief editors, 10 per cent women
Ghana	Out of 6,000 salaried employees working in the audiovisual industry, 1,200 are women
Switzerland	Of all the people working in telebroadcasting, 30 per cent are women

Opportunities for Women

The women at the conference felt it was important that 50 per cent of educational opportunities should be open for women. Even though a professional position conflicts with motherhood, most women felt it important to have a choice of being to be both a professional and a mother. It was recommended that national laws should address the problems and financial difficulties which cause prejudice against women who choose to have children. Thus, the place of women in society will be clearer.

Other measures were recommended to the Commission of European Communities, Employment Directorate-General:

- Training programs to encourage people in administrative positions to move into executive positions
- Technical courses to familiarize women with production
- Company childcare centres or financial assistance to women for childcare services
- Workshops on non-discriminatory recruiting and training techniques
- Information sessions for women on legal rights and company equal opportunity policies.

In order to grant equal access in the film, video, and television professions, women should be actively recruited, promoted, and encouraged. We also need to pay particular attention to all women who apply for traditionally male-dominated jobs. Factors involving aptitude and abilities partly explain why women are not chosen for these jobs and this is where the difference between men and women becomes very pronounced. We must also consider the absence of women in decision-making positions and see if there is the slightest sign of a new generation at the top of the hierarchy in television and film.

The situation of women in the Quebec film industry is not very reassuring and it is essential to unite the women who work in the industry into interest groups and make them aware of the need for joint action. Only through such joint awareness and action will we be able to direct and produce films and videos without being edged out.

SOURCES

Sources consulted include the Association des réalisateurs et réalisatrices de films du Québec and the Syndicat des techniciennes et des techniciens du cinéma et de la vidéo du Québec for statistics of the last two years. Also consulted were: Gazette officielle du Québec, August 13, 1986, Décret 1172-86; Québec, Ministère des Affaires culturelles, "Le cinéma au Québec," working document, June 1990; Conseil du statut de la femme au Québec, *Le salaire a-t-il un sexe?* Les inégalités de revenus entre les hommes et les femmes au Québec, 1987; *La situation socio-économique des femmes au Québec* Faits & chiffres, Louise Paquette, (Québec, Secrétariat à la condition féminine 1989); Rapport de la Conférence Internationale des Femmes des professions de l'audiovisuel, Berlin 1989; Status of Women Committee, *Étude sur la situation des femmes de la Fédération nationale des communications*, Novembre 1989; *Communautés Européenne*, Direction Générale de l'Emploi, Documentation No. 23.

IOLANDE CADRIN-ROSSIGNOL
AND LOUISE LAMARRE

8 Talking to Quebec Women in the Media

Upon reading the *Statistical Profile of Women in the Canadian Film and Television Industry*, we came up with the idea of conducting a series of interviews to find out what it's *really* like for women in the Quebec industry. We studied the statistical data and then drew up a list of approximately 30 women working in the following areas, both public and private; production, administration, management, creation, technical work, distribution, and advertising. Twelve women agreed to participate in our study. This document is a report of their comments.

The point that really stands out is that all of these women succeeded because of their unfailing passion for their work and in spite of the covert hatred for women in our sophisticated industry. All have also more or less managed to maintain a precarious balance between their professional and private lives. However, a striking majority of these women consider themselves to be working "for" rather than "on" a production, project, agency, or cause. This is undoubtedly the reason why many more women work in jobs related to management and production than in creative roles where they would have to spend a lot of time and energy defending their "ego." This leads us to vital questions about creating new avenues.

Only one of the women we interviewed actually wanted to work in the film industry since she was eight years old. Most of the women thought of arts in the broad sense of the word – theatre, art, and literature. It is important to note that at least 25 per cent of these women were interested in psychology. One woman who wanted to become a lawyer first ended up as a legal secretary because she didn't have the money for law school. Another one who wanted to become a nun became a director! Most of the women we spoke with started working at a young age – almost always before they finished their education. They worked in various jobs including sales clerk in the sports department, waitress in a bar, supervisor of tennis equipment at a sports club, attendant for mentally handicapped people, credit clerk at an insurance company, graphic designer, gas station attendant, and even film critic! Whether by coincidence or not, all of these jobs entail dealing with the public.

DEVELOPMENT

Film – One of the Last Apprenticeship Trades?
One thing is certain – before you start working in the film and television industry, you have to learn. Half the women we interviewed first had a B.A. in communications. The other half learned the basics on the job, starting as an assistant and working in almost all production fields. Even though an educational background in communications makes it easier to enter the film and television industry, the fact remains that all but two women, worked also as assistants for a certain period of time. Did the people they work under as assistants or apprentices provide good role models? Although this wasn't true in all cases, people learn just as much, if not more, by making an effort not to make the same mistakes as others.

A Foot in the Door
All of the women agreed that it doesn't matter how you get a job in the industry. The important thing is that once you're in, you're there to stay. Even if times are tough and you have to start from the bottom again and again, it's worth it. These women are motivated by their unfailing love for their work. It is a flame that never goes out.

Film director, private sector Why do I go on? I ask myself that question every day. There's no other job that interests me as much. I have this sort of belief that there are important things to be said through film a little bit at a time. We want to make people think.

Film and television producer, private sector Once you start working in the film industry, it's very hard to leave – unless you really aren't cut out for it. I really loved the fact that I could work as a freelancer. I loved the independence. ... I always loved working on a team. Team work is really what film is all about. Even in production, you work as a team.

Security and Tough Times
This industry experiences extreme fluctuations on a regular basis. Often you have to look for your bread and butter elsewhere to come back stronger and literally change your destiny. Freelancers know all about this topic. Almost all of them have had to cross this bridge at one time or another in their career. You take another job, work in a totally different field, or agree to work for next

to nothing if your husband or friends are understanding and support you. Some of the toughest years for the industry were 1976, 1982, and 1990.

Film and television producer, private sector There was a slow period in film at the same time as the Olympic Games ... Several of us worked on the opening and closing ceremonies.

Advertising producer, private sector 1982 was the slackest period in advertising. Nothing was going on, absolutely nothing.

Film director, private sector Right now, I'm going through a really tough time ... It's very very difficult for me to make my films. My scripts aren't very marketable. If people generally like my script, the directors aren't too keen on it. There's a lot of fishy business going on behind the scenes and the plain truth is that it's harder to succeed if your script features very strong female characters ... I always think we're back in the Middle Ages when I hear people say that a film is intellectual and feminist. I consider these to be two good qualities. As far as I'm concerned, it's women who think and it's true there aren't many of them in film ... And there are also cases when men are the weaker sex ... It's all fiction. I don't intend to make documentaries. I find it a bit sad that I'm confronted with this kind of situation and I would be very surprised if a lot of questions were asked in the opposite case. It's so basic. I thought we were above all that. I thought we could move on to other things. I'm a bit shocked.

Stubbornness and Audacity
The most important ingredients for success turn out to be stubbornness and audacity. Self-confidence is obviously a prerequisite. Freelancers get a lot of practice.

Advertising producer, private sector When you're working as a freelancer, you can't count on anyone. You can't be passive. You're forced to get going, to be smart and to really move. And you obviously learn a lot in the different jobs you take. You get to know a whole new world – you've got a new boss, a new client, a new methodology, a new team. This also makes you daring. Whether you want to be or not, after going through 25 employers in one year, you get pretty gutsy.

Awards
Recognition in the industry is also a great motivator. For example, even if winning awards doesn't guarantee instant fame, it certainly does open a lot of doors.

Film and television producer, private sector Awards certainly help and they look good on your résumé. It's obvious that the award is for outstanding work. That's comforting and yes, it does help. You find that you're a bit better known for it. But what has helped me the most over the years in all the jobs I've held has definitely been the people and the experience.

Contact with people working in the industry, talent, quality work and a very very lucky break are the other ingredients.

How Imagination Fits In

Whether the women work in the administrative, creative, or sales aspect of production, they all use their imagination in their work to solve problems. They all need original ideas to do their jobs, for instance, to recognize a good script, to manipulate figures, to develop funding and implementation strategies, to centre images with the atmosphere of the scene being filmed, to form an efficient production team, to plan the production and shoot the script on paper and then implement it on the set, and, finally, to improvise whenever necessary.

Federal funding agency employee In the approach, yes. You simply can't treat one project the same as any other. First you read the script and right from the start you either like it or not. So, whether you want to or not, even if you have figures to work with, a film that's behind schedule remains there. I don't personally play a part in the creative aspect of film history, but it's definitely the content which enables me to study the figures and say – ok, it's worth this much or it's not worth that much and to find ways and solutions so that the producer makes it and succeeds in making the film.

Constraints

Many constraints also force the women we interviewed to use their creativity. They have to find solutions to deal with or bypass problems and they often have to make compromises. The major constraints include the following: censorship, money, time, weather, personality conflicts, pressure, uncertainty and priorities.

Film producer, public sector, federal Yes, there are a lot of constraints. There are budgetary constraints as well as personality, policy and schedule constraints. The fact that there are only 24 hours in a day and I still have to eat and sleep.
Film and television producer, private sector Working in the film industry essentially means making compromises. I have a project which was refused at SOGIC for political reasons ... In July, the film became reality ... It's a contentious subject. Some of the characters are not very respectful of our institutions and the SOGIC didn't want to get involved. I call that blatant censorship. Sooner or later we'll have to unite and take a stand. That's the side of the job that's hardest to take and the one which makes you

constantly question what you're doing in your field. Every producer questions his or her job.

Film director, private sector I think that the biggest constraint in film is having to please everyone ... It's very difficult to have Radio-Canada tell you that a scene is terrific, the SOGIC tell you it's lousy, and Telefilm tell you it's interesting. Who do you believe?

Television director, public and private sector You always have to respect constraints and sometimes those same constraints turn out to be advantages. There's the time constraint – you prepare, film, edit and produce a final product in a very short period of time. You have very little time to think ... If you have too much time, you start to have doubts. You lose your first instinct. I think that constraints help creativity. The biggest constraint is people's stupidity and incompetence.

Television director, public and private sector The men of my age are easily castrated by the presence of a woman ... When a man uses his imagination, people say he's creative. When it's a woman, she's "gone off the deep end.

WOMEN AND JOBS

The women we interviewed felt that being a woman sometimes accelerates, but more often slows down career development.

Film and television technician, private sector On the one hand, it's been a hindrance to me. At the beginning, I really had to fight. Everyone thinks that you have to be really strong to be a cameraman ... Once I entered the field and proved myself, I got along quite well because people felt I was more sensitive and imaginative. They liked working with new blood – a woman.

Television director, private and public sector The fact that I'm a woman certainly did slow down my career development because there are battles that are not fought on open ground. The industry itself doesn't appear to be sexist. Since sexism is very deep-rooted, you don't spot it right away. You find yourself fighting for something absolutely ridiculous and you keep on fighting only to realize that sexism does exist ... However, the fact that you're constantly fighting keeps the flame burning and you remain enthusiastic and full of life. By the time men reach 50 they're dull.

Film director, private sector I'm from a generation that thought that women had everything going for them. I found out it wasn't true. There is something very subtle in film because the men are very cultured and boast about being for equality and everything else. However, this can only be measured in concrete terms. At SOGIC, when they talk about quality criteria, the three directors who read the projects are all men. They tell us that men and women are equal. Don't make us laugh. When the reports on the script are positive and the projects are refused because the directors didn't like it ... There's definitely subjectivity when the directors are all men and approximately the same age ... It's not right that people like that are the ones who make the decisions about the projects.

Federal funding agency employee I have three faults: I'm a woman, I'm a feminist and I'm young.

Federal funding agency employee It's obvious it's slowed down. But it's not just the fact that I'm a woman ... If I had curly hair, wore a suit and high-heeled shoes, I think I might have gone farther at one time. I wouldn't have had to prove that the short jolly comical person with the wacky clothes was qualified.

Woe to those women who have already worked as secretaries! The job seems to be the stain of original sin that's hard to get out.

Advertising producer, private sector I was trained by the creative director of an agency ... When I wanted to change my title from secretary to junior producer, my boss wasn't thrilled. I was doing all the work, but he didn't want to give me the title. I was forced to leave and change agencies in order to move up.

We also made an interesting discovery. The position of producer may be considered "nontraditional" for women in the film and video industry, but, it's common in advertising agencies.

Advertising producer, private sector Strangely enough, 84 per cent of agency producers in Montréal are women. Even in Toronto, all of the producers I've worked with were women.

Advertising producer, private sector Maybe it's because women have more talent at managing budgets? But maybe it's also because women cost less ... Not too many men are agency producers and it's a sure thing that those who are are making more money. They're privileged. For example, if I'm in competition with a man to produce a beer commercial, the man will definitely get the job ... In the world of beer commercials, all people want is men behind the camera and a bunch of beautiful centrefolds in front of it.

In the distribution sector, we noticed that there are a lot of women in charge of selling film and television productions, but few of these women are privileged enough to be in charge of *buying* the products.

Film and television distribution manager, private sector There are a lot of women in sales, but I'm the only woman in Quebec who does the buying.

Women learn quickly and are apparently more conscientious. Their bosses are quick to give them a great deal of responsibility, however these women are underpaid and their bosses justify this by on their limited experience and youth.

Film and television distribution manager, private sector I've always had bosses who gave me a great deal of responsibility despite my age. I cost them less, definitely less than a man, but at the beginning I didn't really have any basis for comparison. People still think that women are worth less ... It's true that I needed a bit more coaching than a more experienced person, but the difference in our sales results was not that great and I certainly did cost a lot less.

There is also the aspect of isolation that makes it difficult to judge pay equity, especially at the beginning of a woman's career.

Television director, private and public sector When I was a freelancer, I didn't know how much other people were making. Then I started working for Télé-Métropole and found out that women had only been making the same salary as men for two years. Before that, men made $8000 more. Even women who had more experience than the men were making a considerable amount less precisely because they were women.
Federal funding agency employee I don't have grey hair, but I do have the most seniority here and people often tell me I'm the best. But, I make the least amount of money ... Is it because I'm a woman or because I'm young?

Sexism
Sexism has made a comeback over the past years. Just when we thought that equity for women was becoming a reality, we find out that things haven't really changed very much. Sexism has only become more subtle and is therefore more difficult to recognize and fight.

Advertising producer, private sector There are macho men everywhere and advertising is no exception to the rule. For example, many directors don't take the role of a female agency producer seriously ... They often try to ignore you, pretend you don't exist and go directly to the designer or the client. When I feel that a director would rather I didn't exist, I make my presence all the more known ... These types of situations happen often and add to the constant stress of producing a commercial.
Television director, private and public sector There are two ways to look at sexism. There's the type that is harmful all the time, especially when it's blatant, and the type when you say to yourself, "I'll forget about it." Just recently I was a victim of sexism and I was so shocked because I thought I was too old for that. The man I stood up to was a real male chauvinist. So he didn't put up with it, he just didn't take it. Afterwards, people said to me, "you should just accept your punishment." I replied, "Why? Because I wasn't very polite to him? No way!" So I handed in my resignation.
Film and television technician, private sector – I've lost jobs before simply because I'm a woman. I remember one case in particular when I was doing the camera work for a documentary. The people there thought that the work would require a lot of strength.

That's the type of sexism that has most often stopped me from moving on – prejudices about physical strength.

All of the respondents belong to or have belonged to professional associations or unions and almost all of them were actively involved in the group – they were either elected to the executive committee or sat on other committees. Three of the women who are no longer members of the associations had to give up their membership because they now work for federal government agencies.

WORK AND EVERYDAY LIFE

Three of the women who took part in the survey are perfectly satisfied with their jobs and plan to continue in the field. The other women have not yet obtained their personal career objectives. As for those who still have a way to go, more than half of them are working to gain knowledge and experience in related fields so that they can eventually produce or go back to producing feature films. Two of the women have even bigger projects in mind and another two are hoping to move into totally different fields.

When we asked the women to give us a breakdown of how they spend their time, we quickly realized that work occupies a very large part of their waking hours ... Two of the women who work the least still put in 50 hours a week. When we asked them to calculate the percentage of time they spend at work, four women said they work at least 70 per cent of the time, two of them put the figure at 80 per cent and, imagine this, four of the women devote up to 90 to 95 per cent of their life to work! Seven of the women invest so much time because their jobs require it. The other five devote so much time to their work out of love, choice or sickness.

Film director, private sector When I take the bus in the morning, I write. When I'm in the bathtub, I read over a script ... There isn't much time for a boyfriend, leisure or plans for a family ... It doesn't make any sense. I don't want to stop and think one day that I spent 80 per cent of my life working and the other 20 per cent sleeping. I always told myself that I have films to make before I make babies. But then I start to think that maybe babies are easier.

Speaking of relaxation, we also have to remember that more than half of these hard-working women have children. The one who holds the record has three children, four of the women have two children and one of them has one child. The other women we interviewed don't have any children, but it's not because they don't want any. Two of the women can't have children, another one wants to reach her goals before she has children and the remaining three are still looking for the ideal father.

WOMEN AND BUSINESS

We were curious to find out if the women we interviewed dealt more with men or women in the daily course of business. If we refer to the strict sense of the word "business," almost all the women agreed that the majority were men. It was no surprise to hear that the people working with these women in administrative duties were still, traditionally, all women. However, two of the women decided to hire men to do the office work. When we talk about production and filming, there are generally more men than women on the set. The men therefore have more representation. Without going to extremes, half of the women in the group said they notice differences in the relationships they have with men and women.

Film and television distribution manager, private sector Friendships develop quicker among women. With men, it depends on their age. I have female friends who are old enough to be my mother. Men who are that age say to themselves, "she's young enough to be my daughter." The relationships are very different.

Federal funding agency employee It's very different – there's a whole different approach. It also depends on the type of women you work with. Some women are very competitive and others aren't competitive at all. I, myself, am not competitive. I want to work as a team with both men and women. And that's very, very important. If you work with me, you have to like me. That's the way it is. I don't want to be better than anyone else – I'm not interested in that.

Federal production agency employee When I work with women, we understand each other. Unfortunately, young women don't see the invisible wall. You don't notice it at the beginning of your career. We haven't seen the end of sexism yet. It would be all to easy to turn back.

Federal funding agency employee At first glance, men seem more "businesslike" than women ... I'm referring to the producers I work with. Women spend more time defending the quality of their scripts, their director, and the whole project, whereas men more often talk about making deals.

The other women are ambivalent and think that it all comes down to personality. However, many of them agree that women work harder at their jobs for a number of reasons.

Film director, private sector Women are generally more honest ... It's harder for women to work on projects they don't believe in. Women are better at defending a script than men and at being officials and producers. There's something different about their involvement. They believe in it more.

Film and television distribution manager, private sector You have to appear really tough at the beginning so people don't think you're naive and a pushover ... It's sort of a wall you build. The more you get to know people, the more the wall disappears.

SOLIDARITY

Cooperation, Competition, or Indifference?
Women in the field who hold untraditional jobs know each other and whenever
possible act in concert with each other in business or personal exchanges. It is
often not the desire to collaborate that's missing, it's the fact that there simply
aren't enough women.

Film and television producer, private sector There's always a certain complicity
among women ... More and more women are working in production. I think that only a
very small minority of women are directors, and that seems to be a downfall.
Advertising producer, private sector In the field of production, you can't be too
chummy because there's that whole aspect of confidentiality. A better word for it
would be respect. There aren't too many of us and you learn as you go along. Each
woman works in her own way so you basically respect one another.
Film and television distribution manager, private sector With women, it's always
either collaboration or indifference. There's a bit of competition because of the nature
of the job. But there's also cooperation because you often have to exchange information. You find out about a certain client, if he pays well, etc, that type of information.

Future Prospects
We also wanted to have a look at the women's current job prospects and possibilities of promotions to nontraditional positions. We felt that these women
were in a good position to comment on this issue. The question involved a
hypothetical young woman whose career goal was to have their position.
Would it be easier or more difficult for her to reach her goal today? Before the
women answered the question, they often talked a bit about the type of character required, expectations at all levels, education and, above all, luck. Here
are the comments of the five women who felt that the young woman would
have just as hard a time as they did.

Advertising producer, private sector It would be just as difficult for her as it was for
me, but it all depends on her. You have to be the right person for the job. You have to
have certain qualities and if she has them and she's interested in the work ... God
knows there's a position for her. There are so few of us. We definitely need more
advertising producers.

Four of the women believe that it has become increasingly difficult to get the
position.

Film director, private sector Unfortunately, I believe that it's becoming more and
more difficult because each year more people enter the field but the money doesn't

increase and the film budgets do. The competition becomes increasingly fierce. It's not easy for women or men. I gave an interview to some young students and the advice I gave them was to change their minds before they become too fanatic.

Federal funding agency employee Although some people decide to take early retirement, people generally hold on to their jobs for a long time because it's extremely difficult to find a new one. This means that there are less openings in all fields.

The last two women felt that it is a bit easier today.

Film and television technician, private sector Today the door is open to more women than it was ten years ago. It will certainly be easier for this hypothetical young woman. If she believes in what she's doing and has the talent to be a camera operator, she'll make it. It depends on her personality.

Education

All of the women agreed that it's important to be educated, ideally at a university, in addition to having a training assistantship for most positions. With education and training, you have everything you need to evaluate the needs, collaborate with and understand the various people who work in the production chain. Whether you're a producer, administrator or creator, you have to learn to work on a team and enjoy it.

Film and television producer, private sector You have to start at the bottom of the ladder and learn the trade. At university, you gain knowledge and you find out what you like and what you don't like, but you can't become a producer after two years.

Film and television technician, private sector You really have to want it and practise. There are several possible directions. You first have to start practising in similar fields, for example, the industrial sector, films by sponsors, and documentaries, and then use what you learned at university. Then, when you have something to show, you have to knock on doors.

Advertising producer, private sector You definitely have to know the basics. The film course I took at Concordia is what helped me get a job quickly ... If I understand all of the stages of production and all the technical aspects, then I'm ahead of the game ... That's the advantage I have over all the other women producers who received their training in advertising agencies and often began their careers as secretaries. They don't know the technical basics. Sooner or later, this will hurt them because they remain at the production management level instead of really becoming a producer.

Energy

Television director, private and public sector The reality of television is that you have to go through two years of complete bullshit before you can start to breathe. You have to actually work on a set to find out if you like it and if you have enough energy to do the job. Technical training is important because you need the technical jargon. But you really learn the trade by working in it or by watching others do it. You have to like it – it's extremely exhausting. If you're the type of person who likes to work regular hours and have Saturdays and Sundays free, you better forget it.

What about solidarity among women?
The women we interviewed all agree that this is a major weakness.

Film and television distribution manager, private sector Women have such a need to measure themselves to men that they think it's easier to do so by eliminating other women. They say to themselves, "If I want to do well in a man's world, I better stay away from other women." They want to be at the head of the race. I think older women are even worse.

Film producer, federal public sector The women I know stick together. Because they run into the same obstacles, they quickly learn to stand together. There's also the issue of language. Women's language is much easier than men's when you speak about the trade. It's simpler.

Film and television producer, private sector We certainly don't show enough solidarity. The best example is that there are very few women who have sent me projects – in fact, only two.

Federal production agency employee My god, do women ever lack self-confidence! If we showed some solidarity, we could form a strong group and change things. Unfortunately, some women think that in order to succeed they have to act like men. They act like that because they're insecure.

CONCLUSIONS
Just like the genie in the lamp, we gave the women we interviewed three wishes to improve the situation for women in the industry. We're not sure whether the women were inspired by our last question or if it was pure chance, but the fact remains that five of them wished that women would show more solidarity – that they stop fighting and start helping each other. Some of them also said that they were afraid of women succeeding and an unfortunate trend, whether right or wrong, of feeling edged out. They would like to see these two situations disappear.

We also took note of more concrete recommendations, first of all, with regard to the representation of women in administration and distribution of public funds.

Film director, private sector There should be a budgetary allotment at Telefilm and SOGIC, at least one fund for women. It's incredible that our film industry can go for an entire year without addressing women. When we're told that it's because there were no projects, we know perfectly well that it's not the case. It's true that they make different films. We should make an effort to show this different outlook.

Film and television producer, private sector I'm personally against the idea of reserved budgets. I don't think we'll ever feel equal if we have certain privileges. I don't believe it would work to favour women in that way. The quality of the projects is what really counts.

Federal production agency employee The government definitely has to implement incentives and control measures which not only count the number of permanent employees, but also ensure fair distribution of taxpayers' money. We should also seriously look into the fact that women are underpaid and under-represented in all areas.

Five women used their last wish to urge serious measures implemented to create assistance programs for training and development for women who want to enter or specialize in nontraditional work.

ARMANDE SAINT-JEAN

9 Women in the Media – The Real Picture

Over the last half century, women have made considerable headway in their efforts to enter the public sphere of paid work. This is evident in all industries including the media industry. The statistical report published by Toronto Women in Film and Video is of interest in the portrait it presents of the situation in an industry which had not been studied from this perspective. This portrayal enables us to identify the discrepancy between statistical facts and the impression we have of the situation.

One of the major discoveries of the study is that despite appearances, women's progress in the film and television industry seems to have been relatively slow. All we have to do is compare television to medicine or film to a small private services company to see that this is indeed the case. Although women make up a good half of the student enrolment in medical faculties in Quebec, most people enroled in university film and communications courses interested in technical work, directing, and producing for film and television are still men. In the business sector, particularly in Quebec, we know that, over the past years, women have started the majority of small and medium-sized companies. In an industry like film, we cannot help but notice that women have not yet succeeded in carving out a place for themselves equal to their numerical proportion in the population and that they continue to be a small minority group.

All the same, there has been progress. In a sector like the media, where women have always been the minority, they now hold a significant proportion of the jobs – approximately one-third on average. But we must examine what is behind this statistic to discover its real significance. Women are confined to a few job categories, which often involve duties associated with their traditional role: wardrobe, hairstylist, makeup artist, secretary, and assistant. These jobs are all lower paying, less prestigious, less stable, and offer fewer opportunities for responsibility and promotion.

Women are at the bottom of the work pyramid in most areas of work. The media are no exception to this general rule. The types of jobs in this industry can be categorized into three levels. At the bottom, we have office work, administrative and production support. The middle is the creative level, and the top is management. The higher we go up the pyramid, the fewer women there are. "In 1988 women represented 84% of clerical workers in broadcast oriented companies with over 100 employees; but they represented only 9% of upper level managers."[1] The same is true for the creative positions. Women accounted for only 14 per cent of these positions (producer, director, screenwriter, art director, director of photography, and editor).

THEORETICAL ANALYSIS

If we look at a few theoretical considerations, we can better understand the importance and range of the statistics which portray women's involvement in the film and radio-television industry in Canada.

The Myth of Numerical Equality

The first of these considerations aims at deflating the deep-rooted myth that women are equally represented in this sector. There is in fact a definite discrepancy between the reality depicted by the statistics and the general impression held by the public at large. The general public believes that women have carved out a wonderful and enviable place for themselves in the media. People probably have this impression because on television and in movies they see women in the roles of reporters, newscasters, commentators, or movie stars. All we need is one woman in the limelight and we believe that hundreds of women have also succeeded. Often, the opposite is true.

In Quebec, for example, we find it hard to believe that less than one-quarter of all journalists are women. This illusion may arise from the fact that several women journalists have won an enviable reputation and are very visible in the media. Lise Bissonnette, Denyse Bombardier, Madeleine Roy, Jocelyne Casin, and others make us forget that, on average, over three-quarters of the ordinary reporters in the radio and television news studios are men.

Another factor contributes to what we might call an optical illusion. This illusion stems from the fact that women are widely used in advertising for televised, visual, and audio messages. In this respect, we seem to be returning to practices which we thought confined to past decades. After a relatively conservative period, advertising agencies are no longer hesitant to associate a woman's smile, eyes, hands, hips, breasts, shapely legs or small of the back with any product whatsoever, whether it be a car, beer, real estate, insurance, beauty product, or food. Our eyes, ears, and brain are constantly drawn by these messages which carry a feminine touch. In other words, we could say that it is easy to believe that the media are a woman's world, where there are ''definitely many women,'' because we see them everywhere.

A Slow Walk Through History

Women's entry in the film and television industry has in fact been accomplished gradually and even more slowly than in other sectors. The fact that this industry is at the centre of the cultural, economic, and democratic life of society has probably amplified the resistance that these strongholds have to the presence of women. Women are tolerated, but on the condition that they work as support staff, administrative staff, and secretaries, or remain at the bottom of the production hierarchy. Even today, there are many obstacles facing women who want to break through the barriers and become producers and directors. The same is true for high finance, technology, science, and religion.

In fact, we can state that, overall, the stunning developments triggered by the woman's movement and driven by feminism allowed women to enter most sectors which men had jealously monopolized in the past. But we also have to recognize that the more these areas of activity have the power to manage, guide society, and define the canons of social and community life, the stronger the resistance and the slower the progress of women will be.

The media enjoy influence and prestige in our society. For all intents and purposes, they have replaced the traditional village square where town criers and merchants would pass on the daily news. Today, people turn on the radio and television to find out what is going on in the world and to see politics in action, wars being fought, and borders redefined.

Should we be surprised by the fact that the jobs where women account for less than 20 per cent are the ones which are likely the most interesting, offer the most independence, and contain a certain amount of decision-making power? It is clear that as long as women do not have the opportunity to be involved in the management of this collective life, on a global scale, certain doors in the media industry will remain closed. We can, however, find hope in the fact that change follows a progression curve. Studies indicate that there is a critical threshold, generally around 20 or 25 per cent, when the presence of women in a traditionally male industry becomes irreversible. As soon as women reach this threshold, it is only a question of time before the sector is radically changed.

The fact that certain women – pioneers, we might call them – have succeeded in climbing to the top of the pyramid in spite of the slow process of integration means that the ripple effect will be felt sooner or later. These pioneers deserve even more praise because they did not have the benefit of any role models or receive any friendly advice from women mentors along the way.

The integration of women and their numerical progression depend in fact on radical changes in the attitudes and behaviour of both individuals and organizations. It is therefore wrong to consider the "old boy's club" the only reminder of a past era. The relationships of confidence, complicity, and identification which develop between men who went to the same schools or universities, who have the same friends or interests, remain inaccessible to women. Furthermore, the canons of success continue to be defined on the basis of attitudes, abilities, and values which are essentially characteristic of the male mentality. A woman who strives for a position of power always has difficulty convincing a male interviewer not only that she has talent and ability, but also that she has everything it takes to be a "winner" – self-confidence, assertiveness, motivation, endurance, nervous resistance, the spirit of adventure, and sense of risk. The points of reference generally used to identify these qualities must be adjusted, if not completely changed, when women are evaluated. Few men are aware of this.

We still tend to evaluate women's capabilities on the traditional models and the values associated with female roles, such as compassion, cooperation, service, and devotion. In this highly competitive industry, the woman who has mastered the rules of the game of confrontation or who appears to be a better player at the poker game of competition is viewed with a degree of suspicion.

Continuing Disparities

We also see a remarkable difference between men and women, both in salaries paid and funds granted. Overall, women are almost always paid less than men. The lower the salaries, the greater the difference. In production companies, women in non-union executive positions earn 97 per cent of the salary their male colleagues earn. For non-unionized technical staff, this ratio drops to 67 per cent. Even at the CBC, which falls under the Employment Equity Act, male producers earned 10% more than female producers in 1989.[2] Women therefore earn less than men. The same types of differences are also true for government investment in production.

Furthermore, the fact that there are more women than men in all different categories of part-time and temporary jobs clearly illustrates the relative precariousness of women's presence in the industry.[3] In private sector companies, half of all women hold temporary positions. Where unions exist, however, they have had a levelling effect on salaries paid to men and women. Salary differences seem to be much less pronounced in unionized jobs than in contract work.

Since we don't have any statistical data for past periods, it is difficult to measure the impact of the Employment Equity Act. However, the slight difference between the CBC, for example, and the corresponding private sector, gives rise to questions about the effectiveness of these types of measures. One might suggest that only recourse to strict enforcement and mandatory equal opportunity programs with quotas and strict deadlines will enable us to reverse the traditional imbalance.

INEVITABLE LIMITS

Finally, recognizing the unquestionable value of the statistical report compiled by Toronto Women in Film and Video as well as its important contribution to the knowledge of the actual situation of women does not prevent us from raising questions about how accurately the situation in Quebec is portrayed. Some data illustrate the distinct character of Quebec, although not without some paradoxes. The report states that women represent 28 per cent of members of the Association des réalisateurs et réalisatrices de films du Québec whereas at its counterpart, the Directors Guild of Canada, they represent only 6 per cent.[4] In this regard, Quebec seems to be leading the movement! Yet, paradoxically enough, the report then states that 29 per cent of public sector television directors in Quebec are women compared to 45 per cent in Ontario and 35 per cent throughout the country.[5] This second statistic seems to contradict the first one. It would therefore be desirable if the associations would clarify this point and accurately define Quebec's situation in relation to that of Canada or the other provinces.

Finally, there is a certain confusion, probably because of translation, about using the abbreviation SRC to designate the Société Radio-Canada in its entirety and in its activities outside Quebec. We know that there is a very clear distinction between the activities of CBC and Radio-Canada's French network, the SRC. Since no distinction is made, are we to conclude that the majority of data on the "SRC" in Quebec corresponds to CBC operations in the province?[6] Is what is called the SRC what is in reality the CBC in Canada?

Despite the inevitable limits of the statistical data in its raw state, the report published by Toronto Women in Film and Video gives us a truer and more accurate picture of the situation of women in the media industry. Certain myths remain which must still be proven wrong. However, all things considered, there is proof of slow progress. And this gives us reason to be hopeful and incentive to continue. For the moment, however, the majority of women in the industry are still confined to the jobs at the bottom of the pyramid - the least paid, the least prestigious, and the most precarious.

Nevertheless, we do note important breakthroughs on the creative side and in senior management. This is in fact an irreversible historic trend and it will certainly be interesting to measure the pace of these inevitable changes in the years and decades to come.

NOTES

1 / *A Statistical Profile of Women in the Canadian Film and Television Industry*, Project report prepared by Peat Marwick Stevenson & Kellogg (Toronto: Toronto Women in Film and Video 1990), 7

2 / Ibid., 62, 64

3 / The statistics reveal that the margin for full-time jobs ranges from 67 to 80 per cent in public sector television or private sector radio and television. For women, this margin ranges from 20 to 28 per cent (maximum); ibid., 141

4 / Ibid., 16

5 / Ibid., 39

6 / Some data are difficult to interpret, notably Exhibits III-9, pages 36 and 37, III-10, page 39, and IV-8, page 64.

JOCELYNE DENAULT

10 A Short History of Women in Film in Quebec: Behind the camera but behind the men

A Statistical Profile of Women in the Canadian Film and Television Industry (1990) showed that the number of women holding creative jobs in film and television in Canada and in Quebec is low.[1] Its figures (analysed in chapter 1 by Pat Armstrong) are unsettling and have caused me to look at the history of women in film in Quebec to examine how today's situation evolved.

THE BEGINNING

Quebec women were involved in film early on, and their history is marked by multiple forays into all sectors of the industry. These forays were isolated events for the most part, however, and no real continuity was established. The first woman in Quebec's film history was Marie de Kerstrat, Comtesse d'Hauterives, who distributed entertainment and educational film. The only woman in this field, she more than held her own. She bought her own film prints, planned her tours, and crisscrossed the province between 1897 and 1913 with projector and film. She showed these silent films herself, with her son providing the narration.[2]

A second pioneer was Emma Gendron. She wrote two screenplays for filmmaker J.-Arthur Homier: *Madeleine de Verchères* in 1922 and *La drogue fatale* in 1923. Unfortunately little is known about her except that she also wrote short stories and a play.[3]

As early as 1936, nuns also worked with film. They wrote and shot "recruiting" films similar to what has been considered the first feature film in Quebec (which was shot by a priest). Occasionally they wrote the scripts and had the films shot by experienced cinematographers or their chaplain. On other occasions they did everything, including lab processing, themselves. They also shot films in their missions, schools, and convents here and abroad, and these films are valuable sources of information on Quebec society from 1940 to 1960.[4]

The nuns, unlike the priests, did not see themselves as filmmakers, even though their films, like the priests', were shown in the same schools and parish halls and were an important part of what was seen in Quebec outside commercial theatres. Their self-effacement was due to the relatively small number of films they shot, but also to their practice of minimizing their achievements.

GOVERNMENT PRODUCTION
IN THE 1950S IN QUEBEC

During the 1950s, Dorothée Brisson and Suzanne Caron worked for the Service de ciné-photographie du Québec. Their names are unfamiliar because the films made at the Service often were not credited and because they did not make many. They made three documentaries together in 1958, and Brisson made three others between 1956 and 1964.

Dorothée Brisson states that they did not consider themselves filmmakers. They saw themselves as civil servants whose job was to shoot film, not to make "movies." They worked on all aspects of their films: they wrote the synopsis, took a 35 mm camera with a tripod, and shot images that they would later edit. Dorothée calls this process "creative editing" rather than directing since they would often edit material filmed by others in the same way. They also worked in the distribution, production, and post-production of films. In fact it seems that they filmed only when the men at the Service were busy. They say that they could have been directors had they wanted to, but even without the title they are evidence that women worked in film at this period.[5]

FEATURE FILMS OF THE 1950S

During this same time, people from radio, theatre, and film distribution tried to set up a film industry in Saint-Hyacinthe, a "Hollywood in Quebec," as it was called by some. In these studios and those in Montreal many women found work. They took up what would become "traditional" women's jobs in film: makeup artists (such as Denise Ethier), hairdressers, costume designers (Laure Cabana), wardrobe, and script assistants (a position dominated by Andréanne Lafond). The other occupations in film that today are regarded as typical "women's" occupations were also sometimes occupied by women. For example, Simone Besson worked as production secretary, Irene Zerebko was assistant director (on two films), and three women, Suzanne Girardin, Janine Boisselier, and Georgette Pilon, were assistant editors. Only three women held creative positions: Jeannette Downing wrote scripts, Jean Desprez (pseudonym of Laurette Larocque) wrote dialogue and adaptations, and Germaine Janelle wrote music.

At this time there were not many women and those there were worked in women's jobs: the pattern was set. It was difficult for women to advance into traditionally male areas. When Andréanne Lafond wished to direct, for example, she was told that it was not a woman's job! Although everybody learned their trade on the job, women were automatically hired in jobs related to what was seen as women's interests (clothes, makeup, hair) or in clerical support jobs, such as secretaries and assistants. Some feminist theorists believe that motherly functions were being "naturally" attributed to women in general in the workplace. In my view, women were given responsibilities similar to those they had in theatre and radio at that time. Seemingly, women continued in the traditional paths. Film production in the years 1945–55 mostly benefited the women in front of the cameras. Singers or actors like Ginette Letondal, Monique Leyrac, Nicole Germain, Denise Pelletier, or Monique Miller advanced their careers during this time.

THE ADVENT OF TELEVISION

Television arrived in Canada (first in Montreal) in 1952. Women who had worked in film (as script assistants, assistant directors, composers, or scriptwriters) may have expected to see their creative abilities developed in television production, as was the case with men. Their fate was different. Most women went on assisting and doing secretarial work or were offered jobs where what was regarded as their intrinsic feminine qualities would be better exploited or highlighted: this included jobs as interviewers, or researchers, or talk-show hosts. Andréanne Lafond continued to work in film for a time with her own editing and post-production company, but in the end she made a career in television and radio as an interviewer for Radio-Canada and Radio-Québec.

Television did not alter women's occupations or status. The same patterns emerged again: women were either in front of the cameras or working as assistants or clerical support.

THE 1960S

In 1956 the National Film Board of Canada (NFB) moved its offices and studios to Montreal, which represented an historic moment for all French Canadians employed there. Most historians agree that the roots of the *cinéma québécois* are at the NFB in the battle won by the French Canadians for the right to work in French.

Where were women at that time? Most women at the NFB in 1956 worked in support jobs: secretarial, editing, and so on. A few, mostly anglophones, had creative jobs: Jane Marsh, Gudrun Parker, Evelyn Spice Cherry, Evelyne Lambart, Julia Murphy, Alma Duncan, Isobel Kehoe, and some of their films were even credited in the 1940s. However, there were few francophones at this period. Marthe Blackburn wrote texts, translated, and later wrote scripts. Monique Fortier worked at the NFB in London (1952–53) and Montreal (1956–57) as a secretary; she began editing and directing films only in 1963.

Few women entered the NFB during the 1960s. One of the few was Anne Claire Poirier. After working for television as actress, interviewer, and scriptwriter, Poirier started work at the NFB in the translations department. She then followed what was to become the new "classical" career path, editor (briefly), assistant director, and finally in 1961 director of her own short films.

Other women managed to get hired at the NFB in the new "women's jobs," such as researcher, editor, scriptwriter, and film animator. Some women were brought into film by men, either officially (i.e., for a salary), or unofficially (as invisible collaborators, spouses, and girlfriends whose work is impossible to evaluate). We only know of those who eventually moved out of this situation to make their own films.

1960: An Era of Small Businesses

From 1960 to 1970, television had a voracious appetite for film, and small businesses emerged to satisfy the need. At that same time, frustrated NFB filmmakers established their own production companies. Men such as Jean-Claude Labrecque, Gilles Groulx, Jean-Pierre Lefebvre left, head high, for the private sector. No women left the NFB because there were no women francophone directors at the NFB until 1961!

Women in these small companies (many of which were one-film companies) were secretaries, receptionists; sometimes they were called executive secretaries or secretary-treasurer, but they in fact did essential work. Some learned in this way the trade of producer: Marguerite Duparc produced (and edited) most of Jean-Pierre Lefebvre's films. Here as elsewhere, women were invisible, behind the men.

The so-called "great" period of *cinéma québécois*, the era of nationalist films (films made within the socio-political framework of the Quiet Revolution), was not productive for women. Although Quebecers fought within the NFB to show Quebec on film in French, it was a men's fight and resulted in a men's view of Quebec being portrayed. In his book *L'Aventure du cinéma direct*, Gilles Marsolais noted the work of only two women in Québec: Tanya Ballantine (*The Things I Cannot Change*, 1966) and Bonnie Klein (*VTR Saint-Jacques/Operation boule de neige*, 1969, and *La clinique des citoyens*, 1970).[6] However, his anthology stops before the *En tant que femmes* series, which probably explains his failure to acknowledge women's contributions to *cinéma direct*.

TOWARDS THE 1970S

The creation of the federal Canadian Film Development Corporation (CFDC, today Telefilm Canada) in 1967 encouraged a commercial approach to production with film judged by its box-office success and these returns becoming the critical measure of value. Before 1970, only one feature film was directed by a woman: *De mère en fille* by Anne Claire Poirier at the National Film Board. The CFDC did not change the situation for women. From 1970 to 1977, Quebec women made only 12 films (four in 1976 and three in 1977), and seven were NFB productions (six in the *En tant que femmes* series): these films constitute from 2 to 10 per cent of the annual production of full-length films in Québec.

In January 1971, 11 filmmakers founded a cooperative called the Association coopérative des productions audio-visuelles (ACPAV). The coop produced its own films or did contract work; it also co-produced and offered technical services and production support. Most of the administrators were men, although some women were included. A few women directed their first feature film with the coop: Mireille Dansereau (1972), Brigitte Sauriol (1976), Tahani Rached (1980). Some directed their second: Léa Pool (1984), Denyse Benoit (1986). In this context where women make very few films, the ACPAV (along with the NFB) is the most important producer of women's film. Two aspects of the coop's philosophy explain their participation in women's films: first, it is a non-profit organization, and, second, its main goal is to produce films "reflecting Quebec society" in all formats: full-length as well as short. The latter being the format in which many women work.

1975: INTERNATIONAL WOMEN'S YEAR
Early in the 1970s, the NFB accepted Jeannne Morazain's, Monique Larocque's, and Anne Claire Poirier's proposal for a special film series *En tant que femmes* for International Women's Year. From 1973 to 1975, six full-length films were shot: three documentaries and three features were made by crews made up mostly of women. Each script was based on research with women and the content reflected women's lives in Quebec. While an important event for viewers, the series was also a dramatic turning-point for the women who made the films. A number of women, such as Hélène Girard, Louise Carré, Marthe Blackburn, wrote scripts or directed for the first time.

During this time, many women worked at the NFB, although some were there only on a short-term basis. Marilu Mallet, Diane Létourneau, Francine Prévost, Dagmar Gueissaz Teufel, Diane Beaudry all worked for the NFB during this time.

Studio D
Francophone women at the NFB, afraid of being ghettoized, always insisted upon working on regular productions (even though it might be on special programs or series); anglophone women took advantage of the positive spirit

towards women generated by International Women's Year and asked for their own studio. Studio D was created in 1974 headed by Kathleen Shannon. Studio D has two goals: to give women access to filmmaking and to permit the expression of their point of view. Documentaries produced by Studio D (not only in Quebec but all over Canada) examine controversial subjects in Canadian society. Intended to reach women on topics that interest them, the films are meant to promote discussion and provoke change or evolution. The numerous prizes won by Studio D films, locally and abroad, testify to their quality and to the interest in the topics covered by the women at the studio.

Post-1975: Stagnation

In the late 1970s and early 1980s, increasing numbers of women who had come in contact with the film industry wished to continue to work in it. Their only means of doing so was the one men had used in the 1960s: they could start their own businesses, alone or with men. The latter alternative appeared to be the more viable because investors seemed to fear women-only companies; they wanted the women to be endorsed by men.

Between 1975 and 1979, production companies in Quebec increased in number from 92 to 147. Companies jointly directed by men and women rose from 24 to 40. (The influence of women in these companies can also be seen by looking at the number of women in senior management, such as vice-presidents or secretary-treasurers, which may also indicate jointly directed companies.) Four companies headed by women were also founded: Cinemanima (Marie-Thérèse Bournival and Nicole Catellier), the Centre la femme et le film (Hélène Doyle, Nicole Giguère, and Hélène Roy), Productions Agora inc. (Nicole Boisvert) and Productions de l'Envol (Sylvie Groulx). These women decided to take control of their film production.

Still another alternative was the cooperative. This was the choice in 1982 of a group of university film graduates, men and women, who established Main Film with the sole objective of giving its member access to cameras and equipment. The coop produces long but also many short films, which critics see as an explanation for the large proportion of women in the coop. It appears to be characteristic of the 1980s: women mostly make short and medium-length films and documentaries. It is important to note that these formats have the lowest budgets!

The establishment in 1977 of the Institut québécois du cinéma (whose mandate was taken up in 1988 by the Société de développement des industries culturelles du Québec or SOGIC) seems to have been beneficial initially since women's production rose to 20 per cent of all production. However, the level of women's film production soon fell to 15 per cent and remains at this level today.

VIDEO AND TELEVISION

Video played an important role in the history of women in film in Québec in the early 1970s, and it still does today, since it is often seen as a way of making one's name as a director. Perhaps unlike the situation elsewhere, video production is very diverse in Quebec and includes experimental art videos as well as documentaries, news reports, and fiction. Originally video had the reputation of being a cheap substitute for film, and some explain the large number of women working in video by its relative cost. Today, however, video is more sophisticated and versatile and can be considered a medium of choice.

THE SITUATION TODAY

The situation today is probably the most difficult to describe. We are too close to it, and we know little about what is going on.

The lack of information is partly due to the way unions, associations, and trade groups tally their members and activities without taking gender into account, but we do know that women's participation in many of these groups is low. The NFB recently published a list of women technicians in film which proves this point. It lists six camerawomen whereas NABET lists only one. We also lack information on non-unionized sets and we know that there are many.

In general, people in the trade talk of equal participation of women and men because they note women's presence on set. In fact, if participation were equal, women's presence would go *unnoticed*. As far as directors are concerned, the Fédération professionnelle des réalisateurs et réalisatrices de télévision et de cinéma has 110 women among its 500 members, and the Association des réalisateurs et réalisatrices du Québec counts 32 women in its 113 members, a percentage of 22 to 28 per cent; the *Statistical Profile* gave 16 per cent as its figure. The numbers change but the reality does not: fewer women than men direct films. The amounts invested in film production by government agencies confirm the underrepresentation: Telefilm invested 9 per cent and SOGIC 16 per cent in women's films in 1987-88. If 35 per cent of the people said to be working in film are women, these women are not directing: they work as hairdressers, wardrobe designers, editors, researchers, and assistants of all sorts.

And what films do these women make? In television: children's programs and variety shows; in film: documentaries (30 per cent of the annual production), short and medium-length films, but few feature films (7 per cent in 1990). This leads us to conclude that women have to "do more with less": in 1989, SOGIC invested 10.36 per cent of its moneys in women's productions which represented 14 per cent of the productions it invested in.

The NFB's Equity Program has improved the situation but its activities distort the true picture while improving the figures. The program works towards increasing the presence of women in all sectors of activities and it has organized numerous training workshops and programs in non-traditional occupations to facilitate women's access to them. Studio D is also still active and even opened its doors to some new names during the last few years. On the francophone side, the program *Regards de femmes*, begun in 1986, offers women the opportunity to direct but also to work in any position on the film crew. Josée Beaudet, its founder, thinks of her program as "a door on which any woman can knock, and bring her technical and professional knowledge without being penalized by the fact that she is a woman." As of spring 1991 it had 16 productions and seven co-productions to its credit. Furthermore, in collaboration with Studio D, *Regards de femmes* took part in the reorganization of the Federal Women's Program whose aim is to produce films about Canadian women. Because of the NFB then, there are women making films, but this situation is not reflected in the private sector.

In reaction to the state of things in the private sector, women have begun to organize themselves. In the past two years two groups have been founded: Les femmes du cinéma et de la télévision de Montréal (the Montreal equivalent of Toronto Women in Film), and the lobby group Moitié-Moitié (Half and Half). Moitié-Moitié lobbies at both the federal and provincial levels to obtain equity for women in the distribution of government subsidies to film.

THE FUTURE?

With the year 2000 before us, we must remember the past as we look ahead. Today a few women stand out in film and television in Quebec, a fact that testifies primarily to their tenacity. Historically, the underrepresentation of women can be explained by the socio-political context which gave urgency to a recognition of Quebec's needs over a recognition of women's. But we should also realize that women made a big mistake in trying to get into film by the back door, without attracting attention.

Situations do not change on their own; there has to be a *will to change*. Without pressure from women, men cannot recognize the need for change. We cannot hope to get in "incognito" but only en masse.

Anne Innis Dagg, in *The 50% Solution: Why Should Women Pay for Men's Culture?*, proposes an equal distribution of government money to both women's and men's cultural expression.[7] Women's culture is not just that of the women who are involved in the creative end of cultural activities. Women constitute 50 per cent of the public. Women in film, video, and television have a social responsibility to all the other women in this country to get what should be ours: 50 per cent.

NOTES

1 / *A Statistical Profile of Women in the Canadian Film and Television Industry*, Project report prepared by Peat Marwick Stevenson & Kellogg (Toronto: Toronto Women in Film and Video 1990)

2 / Germain Lacallse (Serge Digou coll.), *L'Historiographe: les débuts du spectacle cinématographique au Québec*, Les Dossiers de la cinémathèque 15 (Montréal: Cinémathèque québécoise/Musée du cinéma 1985)

3 / D. John Turner, "Dans la vague des années 20: J-Arthur Homier," in *Perspectives*, Montréal, *La Presse*, starting 26 Jan. 1980, 22 (4): 2-5

4 / Personal research, unpublished

5 / Interview with the author, Quebec, 2 June 1980

6 / Gilles Marsolais, *L'Aventure du cinéma direct* (Paris: Seghers 1974)

7 / Anne Innis Dagg, *The 50% Solution: Why Should Women Pay for Men's Culture?* (Waterloo, Ont.: Otter Press 1986)

KAY ARMATAGE

11 A Brief History of Women Filmmakers in Canada

If the history of Canadian cinema is largely unknown, the history of Canadian women's cinema remains a blank canvas, ignored by mainstream film historians and cross-hatched only sporadically here and there by a few feminist scholars. This dearth of scholarship on women filmmakers is by no means accidental: it is directly linked to the paucity of women teaching and writing about film in academic institutions and power in the media. It is also related to the institutional supports for women filmmakers through the government granting agencies and in the dominant industrial areas of production, distribution, and exhibition.

Nevertheless, women filmmakers made their mark early in the history of Canadian cinema. The novelty of the medium in its pioneering period, combined with its status as a popular entertainment growing alongside vaudeville and the ''legitimate'' theatre – terrains already occupied by women – resulted in a period marked (albeit briefly) by the presence of women in relatively significant numbers. A few women were able to work alongside men in creative positions, especially as performers, but also as screenwriters, editors, producers, and directors.

By the end of the silent period, the number of women in cinema would decrease dramatically with the monopoly practices that accompanied the coming of sound, the rise of the large Hollywood studios, and the founding of the powerful technicians' unions that were dominated by organized crime and admitted only men to their membership. The careers of these women pioneers, however, are both interesting and instructive.

Nell Shipman, who was born in Victoria, B.C. in 1892, is an exemplary figure, for her story parallels the entry, participation, and exclusion of women filmmakers from cinema in first stage of film history. She began her career at the age of 13 as an actress with a small touring company. Five years later she was a leading lady, and had become impresario Ernest Shipman's fourth wife. She wrote, directed, and starred in a number of films, including David Hartman's *Back to God's Country* (1919). This magnificent adventure set in the Canadian north features Nell as the classic heroine, saving her invalid husband's life and bringing the villains to justice through her rapport with animals and her bravery, fortitude, and wilderness acumen. Despite the film's box-office and critical success, however, Nell Shipman's partnerships with her producer/husband and with writer James Oliver Curwood ended.

In 1921 she formed her own company, Nell Shipman Productions, and located in Upper Priest Lake, Idaho. Living in a log cabin 21 miles from the nearest road and 50 miles from a railway line, she made movies independently. Her landscape and her characters were Canadian or facsimiles in these wilderness dramas. Shipman wrote, directed, and starred in a series of two-reelers and at least two more feature films, *The Grub Stake* (1921) and *Something New* (1923), using a skeleton crew, doing her own stunts, wrangling the animals (she was famous already for her zoo of wild animals), and supervising the editing. When the films were finished, she snow-shoed across the frozen lake to the nearest town and put on a vaudeville-type show at the local hall to raise money for her train fare to New York, where she would sell the films for distribution. By the mid 1920s, however, the exhibition and distribution circuits were being closed down by the monopoly practices of the rising studios. After her production company collapsed, she married a third time, and supported herself as a screenwriter for the duration of her career. Nell Shipman's career trajectory thus parallels not only the history of the silent cinema itself, but also represents in microcosm the history of women's participation in the industry. Like most of the independent producers of the silent era, she was wiped out by the rise of the Hollywood studios and their monopoly control of production, distribution, and exhibition, and, like other creative women of the silent period, she was excluded from the all-male technicians' unions (and therefore the profession) which were founded along with the rise of the studios. Later she wrote scripts for other studios. Scriptwriting was an area of filmmaking that always seemed to welcome women. She died in Los Angeles, "broke to the wide," as she put it, but refusing to accept welfare.[1]

Donna Conway King also made her career in the fledgling Canadian film industry. Her story, while not as melodramatically heroic as Nell Shipman's, provides another model for what was to become, in later decades, a more typical career pattern. From 1923 to 1934 she worked for the Ontario Motion Picture Bureau, a provincial agency with a mandate to produce educational films for Ontario farmers. Beginning as a stenographer, she worked her way through producer/director's assistant and editor, to become a director herself. Through the vicissitudes of the shifting film industry, she ended her career as a writer in the publicity department, and left the paid labour force when she married.[2]

May Watkis was one of the few women to make it into mainstream film history. In 1913 she applied for the position of film censor in British Columbia. Turned down in favour of a man, she applied to be his assistant. He agreed, but only if she would be his projectionist, but the projectionists' union in British Columbia and in Washington State argued against teaching women "men's jobs" so she surreptitiously persuaded a projectionist friend to teach her the technique. Watkis later worked in California in the script departments of Hollywood companies, and in 1919, when the B.C. Educational and Patriotic Film Service was established, she was appointed head.[3]

A few basic patterns are already emerging. Women need ingenuity, determination, charisma, creativity, and stamina to overcome the barriers thrown in their way in the film industry. It helps also if they have special talents so that they can create their own vehicles.

The National Film Board played a crucial part in the development of film in Canada and in the role of women in the Canadian film industry. The board was established in 1939 under the direction of John Grierson, and it not only produced films but established distribution offices in hundreds of communities across the country. Grierson hired talented women at all levels of film production, particularly during World War II when there was a shortage of available men.[4] Still, women in the Board tended to be confined to short documentaries and children's films (for which they were paid far less than the men filmmakers), and the animation of native legends.

Women's careers were also affected both advantageously and disadvantageously by another Grierson policy – that NFB films carry no production credits since they were to have been collectively produced.[5] In this environment, there could be no impediment to a woman's advancement if she were succeeding alongside men, and no one woman's failure could be used to block another's opportunity. The group of women filmmakers hired by Grierson, with one exception, remained fiercely loyal to him as a result of these opportunities, long after most had been eased out of the Film Board or out of the industry. The disadvantage of the policy was that women were unable to point out their achievements, and thus were vulnerable to post-war "cutbacks." For the historian, it is almost impossible to delineate precisely the work done by women on films made in the war years. Nevertheless, there are a few women whose careers can be traced.

Gudrun Parker (b. 1920) directed educational films such as *Vitamins A, B, C, and D* from 1940 on, eventually becoming head of the educational unit. She came into her own with *Listen to the Prairies* (1945) and *Opera School* (1952), when her characteristic style using dramatization in documentary was allowed to blossom. Her films are classics of their period. After the war she found herself out of a job and raising a family, and did not return to filmmaking until

1963, this time as president of her own production company, Parker Films. Her career has been intermittent since, although in the 1980s she was still vying for commissions and projects.

Jane Marsh (b. 1915) was one woman at the NFB who did object to the clear discrimination against women. She achieved considerable success as editor, researcher, and director, and was one of the few women actively involved in making war films at a decision-making level. Writing, directing, and editing four films in a two-year period, she became *de facto* producer of the "Canada Carries On" series after producer Stuart Legg left the board. One of her films, *Alexis Tremblay, Habitant* (1943), became one of the most used films in NFB history, still being booked over 30 years after it was made. Despite her position of strength in the unit, Grierson refused to promote her.[6] After leaving the NFB, Marsh worked until 1948 as a scriptwriter and editor for British Information Services in New York. She then abandoned filmmaking to become a professional artist and teacher.[7]

Despite the contradictions inherent in the working conditions for women at the NFB, its unique situation as the principal source of pre-television films in much of the country gave those films and filmmakers an opportunity to make a profound mark on the culture. Thus for Canadians who grew up in the first decades after the war, films by women such as *Peoples of the Potlatch* (Laura Boulton, 1944), *Terre de Nos Aieux* (Jane Marsh, 1943), and *Glooscap Country* (Margaret Perry, 1961) have become part of our collective cultural unconscious. Moreover, the board was virtually the only training ground for women in the profession, and the single source of permanent employment for women filmmakers in the country, employing for over twenty-five years such staffers as Anne-Claire Poirier (b. 1932) and Kathleen Shannon (b. 1935). To a certain extent, such women filmmakers were able to generate their own projects and they enjoyed the luxury of production budgets that were consistently higher than any independent woman in the private sector could ever dream of. And in 1975, the NFB created a new opportunity for women filmmakers with the founding of Studio D, a section dedicated to making films by and about Canadian women.

Of all the films emerging from the National Film Board of Canada in the 1980s, *Not a Love Story* (Bonnie Sher Klein, 1980) and *If You Love This Planet* (Terri Nash, 1981) have undoubtedly left the deepest impressions on a broad spectrum of viewers. Years after their release, they remain the most frequently booked films in the NFB catalogue. Both films are productions of Studio D, the NFB women's unit founded in 1974 by Kathleen Shannon, the first woman executive producer at the film board. She has encouraged the work of many women filmmakers and has generated the production of films on feminist, environmental, and peace issues, believing that films should be used as catalysts for change and that they should appeal to a wide range of viewers. From a shoestring budget of $100,000 in 1974 to the present $1.5 million, Studio D has managed to support a permanent staff of women filmmakers, numerous independent projects and technical training programs, and to produce some 100 documentaries. Under the direction of Kathleen Shannon's successor Rina Fraticelli, Studio D has become predominantly a freelance studio for training and production with disadvantaged, visible minority, and young women filmmakers. It has thus become one of the major sources of films by women of colour and about black and native issues in Canada.

Studio D is clearly a success story for women filmmakers, yet it has become a kind of ghetto for women at the NFB, left behind in the 1980s move into the production of more high-profile feature films, most of which are produced and directed by men at the board. Women remain, 50 years after the founding of the NFB under Grierson, making short documentary and children's films which have lower budgets, smaller crews, and less opportunity for financial return.

Memories of childhood in Canada are populated with animated images produced by Canadian women. In the 1950s, our cultural heritage was recounted in animations of native legends such as *How the Loon Got Its Necklace* (Judith Crawley, 1954), *Kumak the Sleepy Hunter* (Alma Duncan, 1955), and *Legend of the Raven* (Judith Crawley, 1957). Evelyn Lambart created classics such as *L'Histoire de Noel* (1973) and *Mr. Frog Went A-Courting* (1974) after working for many years as assistant to Norman Mc-Laren. And also in the 1970s, a bright new star began to shine in the delightful and always innovative films of Caroline Leaf (*Le Mariage du Hibou*, 1975; *The Street*, 1976; *Metamorphosis of Mr. Samsa*, 1977). The heyday of animation at the NFB seems to have ended, however, with McLaren's death. Women no longer appear as directors of animated films, although most of the studio colourists and behind-the-scenes workers are still women.

In television and independent documentary as well, women filmmakers have become central to our experience of Canadian culture, despite the forces of systemic discrimination documented in the *Statistical Profile*.[8] As in the feature film industry, Canada's television networks are dominated by American programming, but Canadian networks have been successful nationally in current affairs and documentary reporting. Although women have largely been confined to daytime and children's programming, in the flagship areas of current affairs there have been a few women, such as Beryl Fox (b. 1931), who have carved out permanent niches in Canadian television history. For years one of Canada's most innovative and politically committed documentary filmmakers, Fox made key contributions to the development of television current affairs in the 1960s. She joined the Canadian Broadcasting Corporation as a script assistant and researcher, and co-directed her first film in 1962. Particularly in historically significant investigative series such as ''Document'' and ''This Hour Has Seven Days,'' she was a major figure both onscreen and behind the camera. She was the first Canadian to examine American racial tensions, feminism, and the Vietnam War. Although she left CBC in 1966, she continued to make documentaries for television, until she began to produce feature fiction films for theatrical markets in the late 1970s.

In the independent sector, Holly Dale (b. 1953) and Janis Cole (b. 1954) have had successful theatrical runs for feature documentaries. As independent filmmakers who began to work together as students, they share functions as producer, director, and editor. They treat colourful, marginal, underworld subjects in a humanist way. *The Thin Line* is a personal and psychological investigation of the criminally insane inmates of a maximum security prison. *P4W Prison for Women* (1981) and *Hookers on Davie* (1984), both feature-length, celebrate the humanity and survival instincts of women prisoners and Vancouver prostitutes, respectively, and were among the rare Canadian documentaries to do well in theatrical release. *Calling the Shots* (1989) is about women filmmakers trying to break into the feature film industry.

Gail Singer (b. 1946) is one of the few Canadian women filmmakers able to make a living in independent documentary production, and she has been a committed advocate of feminism and socially progressive issues. She began as a researcher and assistant in the late 1960s, but quickly established herself as a director of intelligence in social documentaries on mercury poisoning in Canada's waterways, native cultures, arctic oil spills, battered women, breast-feeding, abortion, obstructive government bureaucracy, and children of divorce, as well as several films about artists. She has worked at various times with the CBC and Studio D, but she manages to maintain an independent profile in Canadian film culture. She has often worked with women as principal crew members, and has recently completed *Wisecracks*, a large-budget documentary feature on women comedians, and *True Confections*, a feature drama based on the autobiography of Sondra Gottlieb.

It is in the avant-garde that Canadian women have contributed most successfully to cinema as an art form. This is partly the result of significant individual artists, such as Joyce Wieland and Patricia Gruben, but their situation has been supported by the funding priorities of the federal and provincial granting bodies such as the Canada Council, which has taken as its mandate the support of innovative and experimental film.

Joyce Wieland (b. 1933) has had a 30-year career as a multi-media artist, working at various periods in plastic, cloth, assemblages, bronze, watercolours, and oils, as well as film. After experimenting with short films for five years, in

1969 she made *Reason Over Passion*, a feature-length abstract film that has become a classic of the Canadian avant-garde. Her colleagues in New York panned the film. One powerful critic, Jonas Mekas, explicitly excluded her work from the newly founded Anthology Film Archives, although later he changed his mind. In 1975 Wieland made a large-budget 35mm feature, *The Far Shore*. The film received a disappointing response from mainstream audiences and hostility from champions of the avant-garde, who saw her excursions into melodramatic narrative as incorrect. As a result, Wieland gave up filmmaking of any kind for almost ten years.

Patricia Gruben (b. 1948) studied film at the University of Texas before moving to Canada in the early 1970s. For almost a decade she worked as assistant, props person, and set decorator at various levels of the film industry. In 1979 she made her first film, *The Central Character*, which uses optically treated multiple images, maps, blueprints and other texts, minimal and repeated images combined with a fragmentary, hallucinatory, and looped voice/sound composition on the audio track. With *Sifted Evidence* (1981), a 40-minute avant-garde narrative combining parody, drama, fictional autobiography, travelogue, and educational documentary, Gruben achieved international recognition. *Low Visibility* (1985), Gruben's first feature-length film, carries on her investigation of the relations of language and subjectivity and of the forms of cinematic illusion, the media of visual representation, and the formations of personal vision. Since 1984 Gruben has been teaching film production at Simon Fraser University in British Columbia, and she has also founded Praxis, a professional training workshop for feature writers and directors. In 1989 she made a bid for the commercial feature film industry with *Deep Sleep*, a film that shows the perils of the transition to commercial budgets, producers, and industrial imperatives.

The reasons for women's recognition in the avant-garde are self-evident. The low costs of materials and accessibility of 16mm in the 1960s and 1970s made the avant-garde a metier from which women were not barred by economic and industrial discrimination. In addition, the labour-intensive, usually solitary, and artisanal conditions of production removed the threat of systemic discrimination against women traditionally found in the film industry.

Another significant factor for women in film is the role of critics and curators. Joyce Wieland's story is deeply marked by her rejection by one powerful curator/critic, and Patricia Gruben's, a decade later, is notable for the degree to which a few feminist scholars, critics, and curators were able to make her work internationally known. The interdependence of teaching, scholarship, criticism, and curatorship, along with decision-making in funding bodies and on juries, is crucial to success in areas where box office returns or attendance are not the telling factors. In the major film festivals, there are only two active women programmers in the country. Women film scholars in Canadian universities number less than a dozen, and those actively engaged in the area of women's cinema are even fewer.

The feature film industry remains the segment of film production most resistant to women. The feature film industry in Canada is hazardous, largely because of American domination of the cinema industry. Distribution and exhibition are controlled by American corporations, and 93 per cent of the films shown on Canadian screens are American. Of the remaining 7 per cent from other countries, 2 to 3 per cent are Canadian. The disincentives for Canadian feature filmmaking are thus enormous.

Within this institutional condition, the situation for women is even more perilous. From Nell Shipman's *Back to God's Country* in 1919 until Sylvia Spring's *Madeleine Is...* (1969), not one feature film was made by a woman in Canada. In the following ten years, 1969-79, less than one film per year was completed by a woman. In Quebec, there have been larger numbers of women actively working in the feature film industry, although their numbers are dwindling along with those of their male colleagues, as the Conservative government in Ottawa withdraws federal support for Canadian culture and opens the doors to American productions even wider with the Free Trade Agreement, ratified on 1 Jan. 1989.

Only a few English-speaking Canadian women have entered the feature film industry since the 1970s. In the 1980s, young filmmakers like Sandy Wilson (*My American Cousin*, 1985), Anne Wheeler (*Loyalties*, 1986; *Bye Bye Blues*, 1989) and Patricia Rozema (*I've Heard the Mermaids Singing*, 1987; *The White Room*, 1990) were the source of excitement with their aesthetically accomplished and economically viable productions. Their numbers remain few, however, in the feature film industry, and their budgets, even in an industry almost completely supported by funding from governments which have an equity mandate, persist at the low end of the industry range. Women filmmakers still account for only approximately 3 per cent of feature film budgets, and those figures have not changed during the past decade.

It is clear that women filmmakers have been most successful in what are sometimes considered marginal areas of film production. In Canada, because of the overwhelming dominance of the American film industry in both television and theatrical features, these marginal forms – documentary, animation and the avant-garde – have been the mainstays of Canadian film culture. Here men have dominated, just as they have in other areas and other countries. Despite their small representation, women have achieved far more than their numbers would indicate. Only the exceptional women have been able to make any kind of mark, and therefore their work has had disproportionate historical and creative impact.

NOTES

1 / Nell Shipman, *The Silent Screen and My Talking Heart* (Boise, Idaho: Idaho University Press 1987)

2 / National Film Archives, Ottawa, unpublished interview by Michie Mitchell, undated

3 / Peter Morris, *Embattled Shadows: A History of the Canadian Cinema, 1895-1939* (Montreal: McGill-Queen's University Press 1978), 149-50

4 / Barbara Martineau, "Before the Guerrillieres: Women's Films at the NFB during World War II," in *Canadian Film Reader*, ed. Seth Feldman and Joyce Nelson (Toronto: Peter Martin Associates 1977), 61

5 / Ibid., 62

6 / Ibid, 64

7 / Peter Morris, *The Film Companion* (Toronto: Irwin Publishing 1984), 30

8 / *A Statistical Profile of Women in the Canadian Film and Television Industry*, Project report prepared by Peat Marwick Stevenson & Kellogg (Toronto: Toronto Women in Film and Video 1990)

RITA SHELTON DEVERELL,
LISA AIRST, AND DAISY LEE

12 Women, Diversity, and the Media

We are three women who work in film and television in Canada. One of us is the anchor of Vision TV and produces its flagship human affairs program. She is in her mid-40s and black (Deverell). Another works for CBC's Disability Network, is in her late 20s, and learning disabled (Airst). The third is an independent filmmaker, mid-20s, and Canadian-Chinese (Lee).

As the *Statistical Profile* amply demonstrates, women are at a disadvantage in the workforce.[1] The long-understood informal observations of women who do this work are backed up by the statistics:

- In the film and television industry women earn less money than men for the same work.
- Women are concentrated in the lower levels of the profession, as far as status and power is concerned.
- Women are little represented in the top creative jobs (producer, director, writer). Only 14 per cent of women are in those categories.

Ironically, in our experience as women who are not members of the majority cultures (English and French, able-bodied) and who work in the broadcasting industry, the dominant factor in our educational experiences, apprenticeships, and working lives has NOT been gender, but race and the stereotypes influencing who can work in our business.

Deverell found race to be the dominant employment factor:

My initial professional goal was to be a performer, an actor, in the theatre. It quickly became clear that only the occasional imaginative director would consider me for roles on the basis of talent rather than on the basis of colour. In the television business, as an on-camera person, I have experienced two major documented cases of discrimination on the basis of race (1974, 1984), both at the CBC.

The irony is that I am a television producer (and paid at the level of my male counterparts for that work). My experience tells me that I became a producer because the path to being a performer, an actor, was closed. The reasons for the performing profession being inaccessible strike at the heart of the experience of people of colour in the film and video industry.

For people of colour, barriers in our industry are not based on sex, as documented in the *Statistical Survey*, but on race. That is to say, the experience of men of colour in the film and television industry is the same as the experience of women of colour. We are underemployed and, if employed, it is usually in the lower levels of the profession.

By contrast, Lee's career began almost 20 years after Deverell's and she encountered discrimination in her education. Her fellow students at Ryerson Polytechnical Institute assumed Lee could not possibly be training for the same industry as they.

I'd hate to put a label on myself, but better me than someone else for me. I'm an independent filmmaker in Canada. There are definite images that spring up when you tell people you're a "filmmaker": visions of glamour and a high-flying lifestyle stir the imagination. "Independent": a strong, willful, charismatic personality ready to take on everything. Now, "in Canada": visions of a poor, starving, strung-out, possibly high-strung, brave-but-foolish soul probably ready to sneak across "the border" with all this enthusiastic support in Canada. Well, if the shoe fits, I'm Cinderella.

Problem: no one believes there's a Chinese Cinderella. Just as no one believed that the nice Chinese girl sitting next to them in Radio and Television Arts at Ryerson was going to make a film after she graduated. If she graduated. Even though she nearly failed the television production course because she got so fed up with her peers for not "hiring" her for those crucial "Six Key Positions" in order to pass, that she created a satire about her production profs as the grand finale to her final year.

My film *The morning Zoo* got made just over a year after I graduated. It is now being distributed by Kinetic Inc. across North America, Australia, and New Zealand, has aired on CBC, Vision TV, and other stations, as well as being shown across the globe in countries such as Italy and Nicaragua, with a possible magnolia prize in China.

Hence, as Lee reports, if she was willing to take the risks and become an independent, the world of work was more open to her than the world of education. Unlike the 1960s, when Deverell started her career, the 1980s brought multiculturalism. People of colour were then encouraged to create work about people of colour.

I have to admit I came into this filmmaking business at a very good time. When I started in 1986, the multiculturalism policy was already set in place. Government at all levels was opening their arms to people like me who wanted to make films about people like, real Canadians, eh?

The multiculturalism policy was supposed to unite the country, not segregate it. We were supposed to think of ourselves as Canadians, not hyphenated-Canadians. The problem with being a hyphenated-Canadian was that, perhaps unintentionally, the label separated us by colour, even if I considered myself a Chinese-Canadian by culture. And although I respected my parents' culture and adopted some of its wisdom, I am still a Canadian by birth.

Lee's and Deverell's histories indicate that the experience of women of colour in the film and video industry is different from white women. It perhaps points to the notion that cultural workers who are members of visible minority groups are viewed very much like white women were viewed 20 years ago, with continuing trickles into the present.

It was once assumed that women could not understand the sum total of human experience, but only women's experiences. Hence we had the era of women working on women's pages in newspapers and being concerned about the home and human interest on television. Women were not as physically strong as men, and therefore could not do the technical work in film and television. Women were not as career-oriented as men, and therefore could not be expected to work the hours and put in the years to become producers, directors, and writers.

Happily, these assumptions about women are beginning to disappear. It is taking far longer with people of colour. It is generally assumed that we are not able to understand the sum total of human experience, but only our minority part of it. This means that the total subject matter of the film and video industry is not open to us on the basis of the assumptions made about us by others in the business. Performing is even more difficult than jobs where we are not "visible." Performers literally represent the entire culture.

For Airst, who is learning disabled, obtaining appropriate training was almost an impossibility. And it has been a long battle to find a work situation to meet her special requirements.

I have a spatial and attentional-deficit learning disability which requires that I receive more than average instructional assistance from my employers when starting a job. I am now in a Vocational Rehabilitational Services training-on-the-job position (with the Disability Network at the CBC). This means that in theory, I receive guidance and instructions at a slower and more thorough pace than "normal."

After a false start in freelance writing, I believe I am finally on the road to a media career. If it weren't for VRS support, I definitely would not have the chance to enter yet alone pursue, a long-sought career in the media. A major reason is that the pace of television is too fast for me to handle at this point in my working life.

As a woman and a person with a disability, the research findings of the *Statistical Profile* represent many barriers which must be corrected if people with a learning disability are to be given a chance to participate equally alongside non-disabled broadcasters.

I have found it quite distressing to learn that women occupy only 6 per cent of trainee positions at NABET.[2] I view trainee and assistant positions as a route for women and the disabled to enter film and television. Women and the disabled will never advance in the industry if they do not have the opportunity to receive on-the-job training. For a learning-disabled person, it is very hard to enter into a media profession without someone's guidance, time, and patience – in order to cope with the deadlines, technical equipment, and overall structure. For learning-disabled adults, the greatest handicap is information processing. However, with the information shaped into an understandable and manageable context, the learning-disabled adult is just as able as her media counterpart to advance at her job.

Women of colour and women who are disabled have stories to tell, sometimes stories that are unique to our ''cultural'' perspective, sometimes stories of the larger society. We, like other cultural workers, should not be ghettoized. Our concern is that the industry become non-discriminatory in terms of training and education, work opportunities, and perceptions of the work we are able to do.

Lee summarizes our motivations in this way:

Here's the real reason I'm in film. I have stories to tell. They're personal stories, rich, dramatic, funny, memorable, and, yes, even commercial stories. They're worth telling, and worth telling well.

Cultural workers who are women of colour and disabled women should have equal opportunity to be educated, to apprentice, and to work in the film and television business. The stories we have to tell, talent, and a desperate desire to do the work should be the only qualifications any of us need. The systemic barriers must be removed. Women like ourselves must be able to achieve goals commensurate with our talent and hard work in our industry.

NOTES

1 / A Statistical Profile of Women in the Canadian Film and Television Industry, Project report prepared by Peat Marwick Stevenson & Kellogg (Toronto: Toronto Women in Film and Video 1990)

2 / Statistical Profile, 33

PAULA J. CAPLAN

13 Sexist Concepts of "Merit" and Systemic Discrimination

Only a small proportion of Canadian films are being made by women, and films made by women in Canada are often described as lacking "merit" or "excellence." Who decides who and what has merit or value? Obviously, in film as in other areas, those with decision-making power, those who control access to resources, get to choose the valued criteria. In spite of this, it has been widely believed that the paucity of women filmmakers simply reflects women's inferior talents. This kind of assumption has been made in every field in which few women are found.

In recent years, new psychological research and theory has impelled many people to leap from believing that women have never achieved much in the way of creativity and genius to realizing that women have achieved a great deal that has not been recognized as excellent or even worthwhile.[1] Until the late 1960s and early 1970s, most people of both sexes thought, for instance, that there had been few or no great women artists or composers of music. With the latest wave of the women's movement came first a *protest* phase: "Here are some good reasons women haven't achieved much"; and then a *revelation* stage: "Oh! it turns out that women *have* achieved a great deal, but we didn't realize it."

In the protest phase, women explained that their energy was limited and their confidence in their ability to produce works of art damaged by the burdens of household and care-giving responsibilities and the influence of the cultural myths about their lack of creativity and genius. Another factor has been the prevalent, powerful (and still-current) belief that a woman artist is self-indulgent and, therefore, unnatural because of being inadequately self-denying and nurturing.[2] In addition, the training and physical materials necessary to produce works of art often required money, and women have had far less access to financial resources. In view of those pressures, perhaps it would not have been surprising if there had in fact been no great women composers or artists of any kind, but that has turned out not to be the case. Indeed, scholars have in recent years uncovered many creative women whose works of art had nearly been lost to history. And we can say with some confidence, after seeing how close these came to being lost, that countless others were undoubtedly, irretrievably lost.

In some circumstances, it could be possible to compose music or produce certain kinds of works of art with little or no money, but the same cannot be said of filmmaking. In general, the materials and equipment, as well as actual production – which is an important part of learning – tend to cost more than for most other kinds of art. Indeed, filmmaker Kay Armatage has pointed out that film is the world's most expensive art form to produce.[3] Furthermore, the outlets for distribution are in many ways more limited for film than for other kinds of art. These factors make women's entry into filmmaking particularly difficult.

In the revelation stage, some critics have stopped assuming that women's creative products have been inferior (and then looking for alterable reasons to explain that inferiority), and instead have begun to ask more fundamental and important questions. Who decides what is great or good art? How do the people who choose the characteristics of good art acquire the power to do that choosing? Why do so many people then accept what they say?

The revelation stage has been reached in a wide variety of fields, but it appears that the application of a revelation perspective to women in film has lagged behind the progress made in many other arenas of endeavour and creativity.

It is widely acknowledged that, in the vast majority of arenas of North American public life, definitions and standards of excellence have been set primarily by white, middle-class, and upper-class males.[4] These standards, not surprisingly, have primarily been those associated with males and traditional masculinity. Thus, for instance, work done with a rational tone and an aura of objectivity has tended to be regarded with greater respect and accorded higher status than work that has included a significant subjective and expressive or emotional component. The former characteristics are usually regarded as male and the latter as female by those who have most of the economic and political power in the public sphere. Furthermore, when researchers' attention is turned to any characteristic and that characteristic is found to be more common among males than among females, it tends to be given a respectful, high-status label relative to characteristics more commonly found in females. For instance, aggressive and self-promoting behaviour has been shown to be displayed more often by males than by females and is called ''assertive.''[5] Responsive, caring behaviour is more often displayed by females and is called ''dependent'' or ''child-like.''[6] Similarly, films made by women are often dismissed as being about unimportant or ''minor'' subjects, in contrast to films made by men, which are often said to deal with ''universal'' themes.

The entrenchment of male-related values has benefited from the focusing of most research on males and the placing of men in positions in which they have the power to define what is desirable and even what is normal.[7] As a result, hiring of personnel and financing of projects tend to perpetuate the favouring of men and traditionally male values and topics over women and a wider range of values, topics, and approaches.[8] The traditional male standard is described not as male or as power-related but rather as absolute, as based on a set of eternal, universal values. In this way, the powers-that-be manage to appear to be awarding jobs and money based on the artist's (or scholar's) and the project's merit while in fact using sex-biased standards and thereby longstanding inequalities. Thus, exclusion of women and non-masculine content and approaches is justified and continued on the grounds that women simply do not deserve the job or the financing; deservedness is determined according to a traditionally male standard, but that inequity is not acknowledged.

The less women's approaches and methods are given opportunity for expression, the more we perpetuate limited approaches and methods as "the canon." Even more dangerous than this shaping of the canon is that male definitions of merit and excellence are treated as though they were the Truth. As Jocelyne Denault has written, "value and merit rest on an appearance of consensus."[9] In fact, it is curious to talk about the Truth of standards of merit and excellence, because the latter are constructs, human-created concepts which humans apply when and as they choose. They do not inevitably and invariably correspond to concrete, indisputable entities. Thus, there are dramatic differences and changes of opinion – by artists, critics, scholars, and the public – about what constitutes great art, good art, or even art at all. Even in the allegedly objective arena called Science, it is now widely acknowledged that there is no Truth. How much more, then, should we be prepared to acknowledge the same for the highly subjective arena of filmmaking and the other arts. And yet, access to resources essential for the creation of films has largely been kept from women because of male standards of "Truth" about the merit and excellence of women filmmakers and their work.

As a consequence, women have made the accurate, though poignant, judgment that, to get a share of resources, power, and success, they have to conform to male norms. The Catch-22 is that, if they do conform, they are condemned for being unfeminine and unwomanly. This is an untenable position for women (and for men who wish to differ), and it has led to the impoverishment of every artistic, scholarly, and policy field. As Jean Baker Miller has written, members of subordinate groups know more about members of the dominant ones than vice versa or even than dominants know about themselves, because the subordinates' (read "women's" in this context) safety depends on their having that knowledge.[10] Therefore, when subordinates' contributions to art and to society are systematically excluded or severely limited, art and society suffer. They are less vital, less richly textured than they could be.

The full and genuine integration into film of standards, subjects, and approaches that have been traditionally classified as female is of compelling importance. It is the healthy course to follow, and it would enrich the world of film and expand the possibilities for freedom and creativity for individual filmmakers of both sexes.

NOTES

1 / Germaine Greer, *The Obstacle Race* (New York: Viking 1991)

2 / Paula J. Caplan, *Don't Blame Mother: Mending the Mother-Daughter Relationship* (New York: Harper and Row 1989)

3 / Personal communication, 1991

4 / Jeri Wine, "Toward a Feminist Standpoint for Psychology," *Popular Feminism Paper Series* (Toronto: Ontario Institute for Studies in Education 1985); Carol Gilligan, *In a Different Voice: Psychological Theory and Women's Development* (Cambridge, Mass.: Harvard University Press 1982); J.B. Miller, *Towards a New Psychology of Women* (Boston: Beacon Press 1976); R.J. Siegel, "Women's 'Dependency' in a Male-centered Value system" *Women and Therapy* 7 (1988): 13–23; Janet Surrey, "The 'Self-in-Relation': A Theory of Women's Development," *Work in Progress Paper* No. 13 (Wellesley, Mass.: Wellesley College, The Stone Center 1985); Mary Gordon, *Good Boys and Dead Girls* (New York: Viking 1991)

5 / J.D. Wine, M.D. Smye, and Barbara Moses, "Assertiveness: Sex Differences in Relationships Between Self-Report and Behavioral Measures," and "Female Superiority in Sex Difference Competence Comparisons: A Review of the Literature," in *Sex Roles: Origins, Influences, and Implications for Women*, ed. C. Stark-Adamec (Montreal: Eden Press 19880), 176–86, 148–63

6 / Siegel, "Women's 'Dependency' "; Wine, Smye, and Moses, "Assertiveness'

7 / Wine, "Toward a Feminist Standpoint"; Paula J. Caplan, "How *Do* They Decide Who is Normal? The Bizarre, But True Tale of the *DSM* Process," *Canadian Psychology* (in press)

8 / Gilligan, *In a Different Voice*; C. Stark-Adamec, "Sexism in Research: The Limits of Academic Freedom," presented at the Gender Science and Medicine II conference, Toronto 1990

9 / Personal communication, 1991

10 / Miller, *Towards a New Psychology*

DIANE SILVERMAN

14 Other Industries/Other Times

A LOOK AT OTHER INDUSTRIES

Canada's labour force consisted of 13,681,000 in 1990 and over 44 per cent were women. Most Canadian women over the age of 15 are employed in occupations that offer low wages and limited opportunities for promotion. That is the finding in the report, *Women and the Labour Force*, released by Statistics Canada on 9 March 1990.

What are the barriers to women? Why are women trapped in predominately low- or lower-paying positions? In the past few years, various industries and professions have studied the participation and earnings of women in their ranks. The following highlights some of these studies and their findings.

Federal Government, Civil Service, and Judiciary

A report on women in the federal government, the civil service, and the judiciary, released 5 November 1990, points out that only 40 of the 295 elected members in the House of Commons are women. This figure, according to the president of the National Advisory Council on the Status of Women, the organization for whom the study was prepared, represents an increase of just 13 per cent since women were first elected to the House in 1921.

The research further indicates that women have less chance of being either nominated or elected to political office, and in terms of appointments and promotions, women are clearly underrepresented. Of the 850 federal appointments to the judiciary, only 73 were women; as of 1 January 1990, 181 women filled the 625 full-time positions with different boards, commissions, and Crown corporations; and, in 1989, in the federal public service, 19.7 per cent of the managerial appointments went to women. Overall, women held only 14.1 per cent of management positions in the federal public service in 1989.

Federal Public Service

Beneath the Veneer, published April 1990, is the report of the federal government's Task Force on Barriers to Women in the Public Service. It revealed that nearly half of the 212,000 employees in the public service were women, yet 75 per cent were confined to lower-level positions, primarily secretarial, clerical, administrative, and program management categories. An environment "which does not readily accept women as full partners in the workplace" was identified as a factor in this situation.

Ontario School Boards

As of September 1988, there were 7385 principals and vice-principals in Ontario schools – only 22 per cent were women. This statistic was released in November 1990 by the Ministry of Education in its fourth report on the status of women and employment equity in Ontario school boards. Many women are qualified for these positions. In 1989, women comprised 51 per cent of those who met the criteria necessary for supervisory positions, and for two consecutive years, women made up more than half of those who trained to become principals.

A discrepancy also showed between the number of female principals and vice-principals. In elementary schools, 18.8 per cent of principals were women compared to 35.4 per cent in the vice-principal's role. In secondary schools, women occupied 11.7 per cent of the principal's positions and 19.7 per cent of the vice-principal's jobs.

The Banking Industry

In the banking industry, in 1988, women's average earnings were 57 cents for every dollar paid to men. The statistic, released in September 1990, by the National Action Committee on the Status of Women and the Canadian Centre for Policy Alternatives, indicated, said NAC, that the federal government's 1986 employment equity law was not accomplishing its task. Other statistics in the report verified that most women in banking still held clerical jobs. Overall, 32 per cent of women occupied non-clerical bank jobs compared to 82 per cent of men.

Law

Women made up 16 per cent of the lawyers in Ontario, according to a study released in 1987 by the Canadian Bar Association – Ontario. Yet nearly half of the non-practising lawyers in the province were women. The report stated that "women lawyers are more likely than men to choose non-traditional careers, and often women spend at least part of their legal careers in non-traditional jobs for reasons related to childbirth and child care." In 1988, 7.6 per cent of the law partners in Ontario were female.

Corporate Boards

What percentage of women have been sitting on company boards? In a Conference Board of Canada Survey made public 1 May 1990, only 5.8 per cent.

This figure has more than doubled since 1984, but the forecast for the next few years is for less growth until more women move into senior management.

Of the 241 corporations studied in the survey, approximately 80 per cent of the women who were members of corporate boards were not employees of the company, but were independent directors drawn from outside the company's ranks. *Note*: No statistics are available on the number of female senior managers in Canada. According to an article in the *Globe and Mail*'s *Report on Business Magazine*, October 1990, individual surveys usually put female representation at well below 10 per cent.

Business Communications Field

The International Association of Business Communicators recorded in a 1989 study that a woman in business communications in Canada earned, on the average, $46,100 while her male counter-part earned $53,900. The business communications field includes public relations, personnel management, marketing, advertising, shareholder relations and community and corporate relations.

Southam Newspaper Group (SNG)

In 1988, corporate management at Southam Newspaper Group, Canada's largest newspaper chain, appointed a task force to investigate why women were so poorly represented in senior management positions.

It found that, in the fall of 1989, 36 per cent of the 7,347 employees at SNG were women. Yet, of the 126 senior managers at the Toronto head office, just six, or 5 per cent were women. Senior managers include publishers, people reporting to publishers and senior staff. The task force made ten recommendations, including to declare "full equity for women" a policy at all 16 dailies.

The Oil Industry

Imperial Oil reported that, in March 1990, 1181 women were in executive, management, or professional positions compared to 841 in March 1984. Petro-Canada said their proportion of women in the same category grew to nearly 23 per cent from 18 per cent in 1986. And Shell Oil indicated that, in 1990, women accounted for 3.5 per cent of the management jobs, up from 2.8 per cent in 1988, and 16 per cent of the professional jobs, up from 12 per cent in 1988.

The Steel Industry

The *Daily Commercial News*, on 27 March 1989 (quoting *The Corporate Ethics Monitor*) reported that none of the seven major primary iron and steel companies in Canada had a female in senior management or on its board of directors. A corporate bias against women was no longer a problem said industry spokesmen. Women were being denied top positions because they hadn't been working at the companies long enough. None of the steel companies would release statistics on the number of women employed.

The Skilled Trades

In 1989, women made up less than 2 per cent of construction tradespeople. Overall statistics are difficult to obtain, but in her study, *Building the Future*, commissioned by the Women's Bureau of Labour Canada, author Kate Braid noted that many women who were employed in the skilled trades in the 1970s, had left by 1988. Yet when compared to clerical positions, Braid found that women derived more pleasure from their work in the trades and were better paid.

Other Areas

The 1986 census indicates that women have made gains in certain of what traditionally have been regarded as male professions. Women veterinarians jumped from 17.2 per cent in 1981 to 35.1 per cent in 1986, optometrists from 17.7 per cent to 32.2 per cent, and managers in the social sciences and related fields from 48.2 per cent to 57.7 per cent. Women pharmacists increased from 41.8 per cent to 50.1 per cent and economists from 20.5 per cent to 28.3 per cent. The professions where women did not make significant inroads included: physicists 7.9 per cent, meteorologists 10.7 per cent, geologists 12.1 per cent, and judges and magistrates 12.0 per cent.

Tables 1 to 4 give some basic data about the position of women in Canada's labour force: how many women there are, where women are working, what the average earnings are.

Facts about Canada's Labour Force

Table 1   Canada's Labour Force

	Males	Females	%	Total
1988	7,422,000	5,853,000	44.00	13,275,000
1989	7,525,000	5,978,000	44.27	13,503,000
1990	7,561,000	6,119,000	44.72	13,681,000

Note: The labour force includes full-time, part-time, and unemployed workers 15 years of age and over.
Source: Statistics Canada, Cat. 71-529, 71-001, 71-220

Table 2   Employed Women in Canada's Labour Force

	Total Full- and Part-time Workers	Workers Service-Producing Industries	
1988	5,368,000	4,486,000	84%
1989	5,508,000	4,620,000	84%
1990	5,624,000	4,760,000	85%

Percentages have been rounded.
Source: Statistics Canada

Table 3   Most Common Sectors of Employment for Women

	Clerical	%	Service	%	Sales	%	Total %
1988	1,664,080	31	912,560	17	536,800	10	58
1989	1,680,000	31	938,000	17	543,000	10	58
1990	1,679,000	30	942,000	17	553,000	10	57

Source: Statistics Canada

Table 4   Average Earnings

	Males	Females
1988	$33,558	$21,918
1989	$35,073	$23,091

Source: Statistics Canada

A CHRONOLOGY OF WOMEN
AND THE INDUSTRY

In the chronology that follows I have included certain key events in women's changing legal status and evolving social, cultural, and employment expectations in Canada. It is in no sense a definitive list but rather one person's perhaps idiosyncratic selection of dates that provide us with a context for our current state.

1824	Julia Beckwith Hart published *St. Ursula's Convent; or, The Nun of Canada*, the first novel published in Canada and the first written by a native-born Canadian
1875	Grace Anne Lockhart was the first woman to receive a university degree, Mount Allison University, Sackville, New Brunswick
1876	Women's Suffrage Movement begun in Canada by the Toronto Women's Literary Club
1882	Toronto Labour Council supported equal pay for equal work
1888	Sara Jeannette Duncan of the Montreal Star became Canada's first woman parliamentary correspondent
1893	National Council of Women established
1896	May Irwin made The Kiss, the first film to show a man and woman kissing
1897	Clara Brett Martin became the first woman lawyer in Canada and in the British Empire
1916	Women win the right to vote and hold office in Manitoba
1917	Minimum wage law for women established in Alberta
1917	Louise McKinney elected to the Alberta legislature, a first in the British Commonwealth
1918	Women given full federal franchise
1921	Mary Ellen Smith appointed to the cabinet in British Columbia, first woman provincial cabinet minister and the first in the British Empire
1921	Agnes MacPhail became the first woman elected to the House of Commons
1928	Anna Dexter became the first woman radio broadcaster in Canada
1931	Cairine Wilson became senator
1936	Nellie McClung appointed to the board of governors of the Canadian Broadcasting Corporation
1937	The CBC broadcast the first women's radio series, Fémina
1940	Women granted right to vote and hold office in Quebec, the last province to grant these rights
1944	Gladys Strum became president of a provincial political party, the Saskatchewan Co-operative Commonwealth Federation (CCF)
1949	Nancy Hodges appointed Speaker in the British Columbia legislature
1951	Charlotte Whitton elected Canada's first woman mayor in Ottawa

1952	Ontario passed equal pay legislation
1954	Women's Bureau established in the federal Department of Labour
1956	Huguette Plamondon became the first woman vice-president of the Canadian Labour Congress
1956	Legislation enacted guaranteeing equal pay for equal work within federal jurisdiction
1957	Ellen Fairclough became the first woman federal cabinet minister
1962	Claire Kirkland-Casgrain became Quebec's first woman member of parliament and cabinet minister
1966	Thérèse Casgrain helped found the Fédération des femmes du Québec
1967	Royal Commission on the Status of Women was set up, chaired by Florence Bird
1968	Divorce Act allowed, for the first time, divorce on the grounds of marriage breakdown
1969	Réjane Laberge-Colas became judge of the Quebec Superior Court
1971	Canada Labour Code amended to prohibit discrimination in the workplace on the grounds of sex and marital status, reinforce the principle of equal pay for equal work and provide for maternity leave
1972	National Action Committee on the Status of Women created
1973	First major brief on sexism in broadcasting was made by Women for Political Action before the Canadian Radio and Television Commission
1973	Canada hosted its first women's film festival, The Toronto Women's (1897-1973) International Film Festival
1974	Pauline McGibbon became lieutenant-governor of Ontario
1974	The National Film Board of Canada opened Studio D
1974	Jan Tennant became the first woman announcer to read the national television news on CBC
1975	International Women's Year
1975	Gertrude Lane appointed chairman of the Canada Council
1975	Federal Omnibus Bill on the Status of Women passed
1975	Grace Hartman became president of the Canadian Union of Public Employees
1977	Canadian Human Rights Act passed, forbidding discrimination on the basis of sex and ensuring equal pay for work of equal value
1978	Labour Code amended to remove pregnancy as grounds for layoff or dismissal
1979	CBC hosted a seminar on the portrayal of women in television

1979	Betty Zimmerman appointed first woman director of Radio Canada International
1979	The Canadian Radio-television and Telecommunications Commission (CRTC) established a Task Force on Sex-Role Stereotyping in the Broadcast Media
1980	Jeanne Sauvé appointed first woman Speaker of the House of Commons
1980	Alexa McDonough elected leader of the Nova Scotia NDP, the first woman to head a political party
1982	Bertha Wilson became the first woman appointed to the Supreme Court of Canada
1982	The Canadian Association of Broadcasters (CAB) developed "Private Broadcasting Voluntary Guidelines on Sex-Role Stereotyping" for its members
1983	Jeanne Sauvé appointed Canada's first woman governor general
1983	MediaWatch, established in 1981 as a committee of NAC, became independent
1983	Margaret Lyons and Thérèse Sevigny become the first women vice-presidents of the CBC
1984	Trina McQueen appointed first woman director of CBC TV
1985	LEAF, The Women's Legal, Education and Action Fund established
1986	Employment Equity Act proclaimed
1986	The National Film Board created En regards de femmes
1987	NFB established an Employment Equity Program
1987	Joan Donaldson appointed head of CBC Newsworld
1989	Audrey McLaughlin elected leader of the federal New Democratic Party
1989	Joan Pennefather appointed first woman film commissioner and chair of the National Film Board of Canada
1989	Trina McQueen appointed first woman director of CBC Television News and Current Affairs
1991	New Broadcasting Act passed

SOURCES

Material on women in other industries was drawn from press coverage over the last few years. Information for the time line was drawn from MediaWatch, the CBC, and the National Film Board, as well as the following sources: J. LeBlanc, ''More Women at Work,'' *Canadian Business Review* 12, no.2 (1985); *Towards Equality for Women – A*

Canadian Chronology (Status of Women Canada 1991); C. Hacker, *The Book of Canadians* (Edmonton: Hurtig 1985); J. Myers, *The Fitzhenry and Whiteside Book of Canadian Facts and Dates* (Toronto 1986); D.J. Bercuson and J.L. Granatstein, *The Collins Dictionary of Canadian History – 1967 to the Present* (Toronto 1988); *The Canadian World Almanac and Book of Facts* (Toronto: Global Press 1991); *Women of Action* (Ontario Women's Directorate 1988); M. Armour and P. Staton, *Canadian Women in History: A Chronology* (Toronto: Green Dragon Press 1990); *Cinema Canada Magazine*, October 1989; *Canadian Women's Studies* 8, no.1 (spring 1987).

Part Three A PLAN OF ACTION

PART THREE

A Plan of Action

THE SITUATION TODAY

When Toronto Women in Film and Television was founded in 1984, one of its aims was to ensure that the public and private sectors of the industry were aware of and responsive to the concerns of women. It soon became apparent that hard data about women in the industry had not been compiled. The *Statistical Profile of Women in the Canadian Film and Television Industry* was commissioned to find out exactly who was working, what they were paid, where and how they were educated or trained, and whether women were benefitting from public moneys going to the industry.

The *Statistical Profile* began the process of answering those questions. Women form only 35 per cent of the workforce in the film and television industry; they are 44 per cent of the workforce in Canada. Women still dominate certain job categories in the industry: secretary and bookkeeper, continuity, wardrobe, hair, and makeup. Women earn less than men across the board. Women producers have access to less money; in 1987-88, according to figures drawn from the Telefilm annual report, women producers received 9 per cent of the total funds allocated for English and French production by Telefilm Canada. Women form 14 per cent of upper management in public sector television/radio companies; in the private sector they are only 1 per cent. In the key creative areas of producer, director, scriptwriter in Telefilm-supported English and French projects in 1987-88 the figures were 10 per cent women producers, 9 per cent women directors, and 14 percent women scriptwriters (*Statistical Profile*, 72).

The statistics demonstrate without question that women remain in the "pink-ghetto" jobs in the film and television industry, that we earn less than men, and that we are outside the positions of power. Indeed the *Profile* demonstrated that women in the film and television industry are in a worse situation than women in other sectors of the economy in that their participation is less. Women in the film and television industry are like women elsewhere in that they are more likely to be found in low-ranking, low-status, and low-income jobs.

HOW DO WE CHANGE THE SYSTEM

It is not enough to point out inequities of employment or earnings and expect that they will be rectified over time. It is not enough to have a vaguely stated policy to work to remove those inequities; universities in Canada have had such policies in place since the sixties, and the proportion of women on faculties has barely risen. Institutions as diverse as Ontario Hydro and the Bank of Montreal are recognizing the existence of glass ceilings against the promotion of women in their structures and trying to find ways to break them. Without absolute commitment by all to change – and ways of enforcing that change – it does not occur.

It must be emphasized that women are not a minority group; we are a majority, 52 per cent of the population. Nor can women be viewed as a monolithic entity. In our number we include every conceivable group. All are at a disadvantage in our society, however, and those who are twice members of the ''designated groups'' in the federal Employment Equity Act – as women and as aboriginal peoples, persons with disabilities, visible minorities – are doubly disadvantaged. This report, like the *Statistical Profile*, looks at women as a whole; to look at the groups encompassed within would be another study. But we wish to emphasize that although the ''other'' designated groups are not singled out in each of the recommendations that follow, their existence and their concerns must be remembered and considered.

A SPECIAL INDUSTRY

Many of the problems that face women in the film and television industry are the same as those facing women in other industries, but the film and television industry is not an industry like any other. Its structure is peculiar to itself. Much of the legislation and regulations that govern our society are designed to apply to companies, particularly companies that employ substantial numbers of people. The Employment Equity

Act, 1986, for instance, applies only to companies employing 100 or more people. The private sector of the film and television industry, however, relies significantly on contract and freelance labour. Currently, most production companies do not generally employ permanent staffs of more than ten people. When a production company succeeds in raising the money to get a project underway – an example might be a television movie sold to the CBC and to an American broadcaster and financed by Telefilm and OFDC – it then contracts with all the production people necessary to produce the film. A film of the sort in our example might have a budget of $3.5 million and require dozens of people working for several months to make it. None of the equity legislation covers these people.

The film and television industry is not an industry like any other because of its influence on our society. It mirrors our society and it shapes it by the images it portrays and the ways in which it portrays them. It is one of our society's most powerful means of communicating with one another. If women are excluded from significant involvement in what we see and how we see it, if women's voices are not heard, if women's opinions and perspectives are ignored, we are disenfranchised.

PUBLIC OR PRIVATE

The film and television industry in Canada, both the public and the private sector, relies in large part on public funds. All of our taxes, women's along with men's, support the CBC, the provincial educational networks, and the National Film Board who produce television programs and films using in-house staff and freelance filmmakers. Private sector production companies benefit from public funds when they sell their programs to publicly funded broadcasters. Public funds also support crown corporations such as Telefilm Canada and its provincial equivalents who act, as their administrators like to see it, as a bank, investing money in and lending money to private sector companies to enable films to be made. But, unlike chartered banks in the private sector, the public sector lenders' criteria for investment and loan decisions are to some extent cultural and, unlike their private sector equivalents, only a small percentage of "loans" are ever repaid. Our money is used to make many of the programs we see on our television screens both on the public network and on private networks. And our money goes to private companies to make films.

ition the airwaves are owned by all of us, and the Canadian
evision and Telecommunications Commission (CRTC), re-
.... .hat notion of public ownership, regulates the broadcasting
industry both public and private. It thus helps determine what we see on
both the public and the private networks. Since public funds are what
supports the film and television industry, we therefore have a right to
ensure that the interests, the viewpoint, the insights of over half the
population are reflected in what that industry offers for our consump-
tion. Throughout its history, the CRTC has never had a clear mandate
to ensure that the interests of women are addressed and consequently
has contributed little or nothing towards improving such things as sex-
role stereotyping or violence against women or employment of women,
apart from establishing vague, voluntary guidelines, holding hearings,
and issuing reports.

PORTRAYAL

In December 1990 the CRTC published *The Portrayal of Gender in
Canadian Broadcasting: Summary Report, 1984-1988*, the results of a
study it commissioned from Erin Research. This study into gender
portrayal and sex-role stereotyping in the broadcast media is the follow-
up to a 1984 study (published 1986) which the CRTC intended to
"assess progress in eliminating sex-role stereotyping across Canadian
broadcasting and advertising industries." The 1990 *Summary Report*
does not demonstrate progress. It states that there has been almost no
change between 1984 and 1988. Fewer women than men are found in
every area, largely because, according to the Erin report, there are many
more men than women in the age range 35 to 65 participating. The only
group to see general change is in announcers and hosts. In other words
licensees have feminized the public face of broadcasting in certain areas
but done little else, and we wonder if this change has not been made
cynically to deceive the public into thinking that something more than
cosmetic has been achieved.

The *Summary Report* reflects a very narrowly defined statistical
study. It includes little commentary or analytical interpretation. Important issues are not addressed. In dramatic broadcasting the study does
not look at whether or not the women's perspective is present. Whether
or not key creative personnel are women or men is ignored. Similarly,
in non-dramatic broadcasting, such as current affairs, there is no

indication of whether or not there is a women's perspective. A woman announcer is not indicative of perspective.

The approach of the CRTC – and others in the industry – is limiting too in its use of the term ''sex-role stereotyping.'' These words narrow our focus to a tiny range of people; we look only at the people who are on the screen. We do not look at the multitude of women never to be seen there. And who are those women we find on the screen? They are in effect consumer products – predominantly young, attractive, of child-bearing age. This is true of the reporters and announcers in non-dramatic broadcasting; it is true of the characters in dramatic broadcasting. The *Summary Report* and ACTRA statistics confirm that once a woman reaches 35 or so there is little place for her on the screen. Wrinkles and grey hair are assets that give men an air of authority; they are debits that bar women from work.

Balance must be achieved in the portrayal of women and men in all aspects of broadcasting and of film. Women must be seen as people not products labelled: Exp. *Better before age 35*. We urge therefore that the CRTC and all those involved in the film and television industry begin to think in terms of ''portrayal equity.'' We need language that expands our horizens, and in our view portrayal equity encompasses the objectives of balance and fairness to all.

GOALS

The analysis and commentary in this document have outlined what the industry and society in general needs to do to promote equality for women in this industry. But the recommendations that follow are not important only to the women in the industry. They are important to all women – and indeed to all men – who want their children to grow up with a full spectrum of opportunities before them and with a healthy view of all people. Our collective vision of the world must include what both men and women see – how both interpret and invent the world.

Our detailed recommendations follow. They outline **how** our goals might be met. Our goals themselves are simple. They are:

- **equal access for women to work at all levels;**
- **equal funding for women's projects, women's perspective;**
- **equal voice for women in describing and determining the world we live in.**

RECOMMENDATIONS:
The Public Sector

These recommendations are designed to allow the goals to be reached by means of several possible approaches. It is not our aim in this document to single out one approach as *correct*. We ask all to recognize, therefore, that implementation of certain recommendations may achieve our goals and thus make others redundant.

LEGISLATION

1   That the Broadcasting Act, given royal assent, be implemented immediately. Its definition of broadcast policy for Canada provides for "equal rights." It states that the broadcasting system should "through its programming and the employment opportunities arising out of its operations, serve the needs and interests, and reflect the circumstances and aspirations, of Canadian men, women, and children, including equal rights, the linguistic duality and multicultural and multiracial nature of Canadian society and the special place of aboriginal peoples within that society ..." The Department of Employment and Immigration, as the department responsible for the Employment Equity Act and the Federal Contractors Program, assist the CRTC in addressing this requirement under the Broadcasting Act.

2   That the Department of Employment and Immigration strengthen the Employment Equity Act, 1986, during its 1991 review, by extending the coverage – now confined to employees – to include all long-term contractual relationships. That consideration be given at the same time to determining how to extend this coverage to all freelance and other similar non-employee relationships.

3   That the Department of Employment and Immigration recommend and the government enact revisions to the Employment Equity Act, 1986, during its 1991 review, by requiring organizations to develop and implement mandatory employment equity plans which include criteria for evaluation and timetables, and to report their progress annually, with appropriate penalties for those which do not comply and meet their goals.

4   That all provinces develop, revise, and enforce employment equity legislation, so that all media institutions and organizations, both public and private sector, be required to develop and implement employment equity plans, which include measurable goals and time-tables, and to report their progress annually, with penalties for those which do not comply or meet their goals. That the federal government should take a leadership role and in cooperation with the private sector should work to ensure a reasonable amount of consistency in reporting requirements.

GOVERNMENT REGULATION

Canadian Radio-television and
Telecommunications Commission

The CRTC is in spring 1991 reviewing its policy on sex-role stereo-typing. As noted earlier, in December 1990 the CRTC published the results of a study commissioned from Erin Research, *The Portrayal of Gender in Canadian Broadcasting: Summary Report, 1984-1988*, which compares data from 1988 with that compiled in 1984. This document reports little or no change in the portrayal of women in the period stud-ied. It is time for a new approach. The existing guidelines should be re-vised beginning with their title. The term ''sex-role stereotyping'' limits the way in which we look at the problem. This term should be re-placed by the term ''portrayal equity'' to open up the whole question of balanced portrayal and treatment of the sexes both on the screen and be-hind the camera. The problem of ensuring that the women's perspective is given equal time and money must be addressed in these guidelines. Once these revised guidelines are in place the monitoring of them must be broadened from the current narrow base to take into account this question of perspective. Finally, the process of overseeing implemen-tation of the guidelines must be revised. The complaint-driven method has not been successful. Self-regulation appears in this instance to be a case of setting the fox to guard the henhouse. Significant improvement will only come with mandatory, not voluntary guidelines.

5   That the Canadian Radio-television and Telecommunications Commission establish as quickly as possible the conditions for licences necessary for implementing "equal rights" under the Broadcasting Act. Those conditions should prescribe the constitution of programming and advertising to meet the definition of broadcasting policy as defined in the act.

6   That the Canadian Radio-television and Telecommunications Commission and the Canadian Association of Broadcasters agree on revised and mandatory guidelines providing for portrayal equity. These would include additional guidelines providing for:

• *Perspective*:
  Women's perspective shall be presented equally with men's both in dramatic and non-dramatic programming. In drama, the perspective can come through the protagonists, as well as through the key creative personnel, writers, directors, and producers. In non-dramatic programming, women's perspective can come through the reporters, experts, as well as the writers, directors, and producers.

• *Employment*:
  Employment of women in key creative roles shall be recognized explicitly as helping to ensure portrayal equity.

7   That the Canadian Advertising Foundation guidelines be revised to include and reflect the guidelines on perspective and employment as outlined above.

8   That the Canadian Radio-television and Telecommunications Commission interpret the words in the Broadcasting Act "employment opportunities arising out of [the Canadian broadcasting system's] operations" to mean that the CRTC must ensure that all licensees achieve employment equity as a mandatory condition of licence. As per the enforcement provisions of the act, the CRTC would have the power to make enforceable mandatory orders, to take away licences or to fail to renew them, or to impose fines.

9   That the Canadian Radio-television and Telecommunications Commission ask the Department of Employment and Immigration to review the relevant reports of all licensees, including those under the existing Employment Equity Act, and report back to the CRTC with an assessment indicating whether their performance is acceptable or not.

10 That the Canadian Radio-television and Telecommunications Commission continue to monitor portrayal of gender and that it broaden its definitions to include data on creative input and perspective in consultation with women's groups such as MediaWatch, National Action Committee on the Status of Women, Women in Film and Television groups, ACTRA Women's Committee, LEAF. To assist it in monitoring the CRTC should require broadcasters to report information about the women's perspective in both dramatic and non-dramatic programming by tracking women protagonists in the first instance and women reporters, experts, and announcers in the second, as well as by reporting on the key creative personnel for both (executive producers, producers, writers, camera, art directors, editors).

11 That the role of the Canadian Radio-television and Telecommunications Commission's internal committee on sex-role stereotyping be expanded to receive complaints directly and to oversee the enforcement of the mandatory guidelines.

Contract Compliance

12 That the minister of employment and immigration direct that the requirements of the Federal Contractors Program be adapted for any contract compliance program and be tailored to the film, television and video field. That it be applicable to all sizes of companies and to all contracts of $50,000.00 and more and to all federal agencies and crown corporations and that its enforceability be expanded. Random audits should be supplemented by a requirement for annual reporting to the government of contractors' plans and workplace data.

13 That all provinces, territories, and sizeable municipalities introduce contract compliance policies so that companies and employers are prevented from acquiring publicly funded contracts if they discriminate against women and members of other designated groups, and do not take steps to correct employment inequities. That the federal government should take a leadership role and work with all parties to ensure a reasonable amount of consistency in reporting requirements.

Information and Monitoring

14 That the Department of Communications in cooperation with Employment and Immigration and Labour Canada direct the public agencies in the film and television industry to create a program with responsibility for ensuring that:

(i)   all sectors and organizations in the film and television industry, including those in the private sector, be required to keep up-to-date records (with data on radio and television separated) on funding, hiring, pay, and other employment practices which include the gender of the recipient, according to a model to be developed with women's organizations such as MediaWatch, Women in Film and Television, and Moitié-Moitié that measures accurately the film and television industry and includes a breakdown of occupation groups such as that used by the National Film Board of Canada.

(ii)   statistics on the status of women in Canada's media institutions are updated regularly to provide accurate data on the participation rate and earnings of women in all sectors of the film and television industry and an essential overview of any change, and released to the public without delay.

(iii)   an up-to-date data base or directory of all the women available to work in the film and television industry in all job categories is compiled including from existing provincial lists as available and distributed to the industry.

(iv)   there is distribution to the film and television industry of this directory of women.

15 That a public awareness campaign be undertaken by the minister responsible for the status of women with support by the departments of Communications and Employment and Immigration to deal with gender bias in the media and its effects on society, and that the minister be required to report to parliament every two years on the results of that campaign.

GOVERNMENT POLICY

Employment and Earnings

16 That management of public sector institutions and agencies establish the objective of equality in all job categories, including senior management, and that achieving equality be part of performance appraisals of senior managers.

17 That management of public sector institutions of all sorts establish as a policy that every short list of job candidates include at least one woman.

18 That management of public sector institutions of all sorts establish as a policy that every short list of job candidates include representation from the designated groups of visible minorities, people with disabilities, and aboriginal peoples.

19 That the boards of directors of the Canadian Radio-television and Telecommunications Commission, Canadian Broadcasting Corporation, Telefilm Canada, National Film Board of Canada, and all media-related boards, commissions, special committees, and task forces, both federal and provincial, each at all times be composed of and maintained at an equitable balance of men and women. We consider a reasonable target date for effecting this change to be 1994.

20 That the president and chair of the Canadian Broadcasting Corporation and the chair and film commissioner of the National Film Board of Canada establish priorities in terms of implementation of production budget allocations at the CBC and the NFB to ensure at least an equal distribution between men and women.

21 That the Department of Communications, the Canadian Radio-television Corporation, Telefilm Canada, the National Film Board, their provincial counterparts, and all government-funded television networks each be required to achieve gender balance, based on Department of Employment and Immigration availability data and reportable annually across all occupations, throughout all hierarchical levels, and should include full staff complement including temporary, contract, and freelance positions. The Treasury Board should be required to report publicly on their equity plans and the current numbers in the public service, especially in these departments and agencies.

Social Policy

Those who work in the film and television industry in Canada face long and varying hours, periods of unemployment, and work away from home. As Pat Armstrong has outlined in her article, these conditions are not conducive to a stable family life, and women and men in the industry find it difficult to combine their work with raising children. Since women still take the major role in child care in our society, improved day care arrangements, as well as changes to the income tax policy, are necessary to allow women to work in the industry and to assume key decision-making roles during the child-rearing years.

22   That the governments of Canada and the provinces cooperate in the development of an expanded child care system, responsive to the irregular hours and needs of the workforce in the film and television industry, with space available for all who require it and extended pregnancy and parental leave programs.

23   That the governments of Canada and the provinces cooperate in the development of extended pregnancy and parental leave programs.

24   That the Department of Finance modify personal income tax policy so that all expenses paid for child care in pursuit of professional jobs are deductible from the taxable employment income of the person paying it.

Labour Policy

25   That the Department of Employment and Immigration in cooperation with the Department of Communications and the equivalent provincial bodies establish incentive programs to encourage an increased number of women in all trainee, assistant, and entry-level positions in the film and television industry. This program should have as its objective moving women into a career path towards key decision-making positions and should be created in consultation with the affected target groups, industry representatives, unions, associations, and guilds. Annual reports on the progress of the program should be required.

INVESTMENT

26 That the minister of communications strongly encourage and the board of directors or appropriate governing body should direct Telefilm Canada and the provincial agencies to establish a means of encouraging applications in all programs from women designed to increase the rate of applications by 10 per cent per year until women form at least 50 per cent of applicants. These means should include a specific mentoring program for women in which experienced producers are signed and paid to assist first-time women producers to obtain financial support from the various funding agencies.

27 That the minister of communications should strongly encourage and the board of directors should direct Telefilm Canada to develop an immediate plan by which, through the use of an incentive point system, the percentage of money distributed to women is increased until it reaches 50 per cent of all moneys in all programs.

28 That the ministers responsible in each province strongly encourage those agencies responsible for allocating funds for film and television production to develop an immediate plan to use incentive programs designed to increase progressively the funds allocated to women until women receive 50 per cent of the moneys available in all programs.

29 That the minister of communications should strongly encourage and the board of directors should direct Telefilm Canada to design an immediate plan to use an incentive program to increase the number of women in above-the-line categories, as well as in non-traditional positions.

30 That the ministers responsible in each province should strongly encourage those agencies responsible for allocating funds for film and television to develop an immediate plan to use incentive programs designed to increase the number of women in all projects in above-the-line categories, as well as in non-traditional positions.

31 That Telefilm Canada re-evaluate its criteria of selection to ensure that any possible underlying male bias is eliminated.

32 That the Department of Finance in cooperation with Revenue Canada develop a five-year capital cost allowance program to attract investment for projects of women producers.

EDUCATION AND TRAINING

The recommendations on education and training that follow are designed for post-secondary institutions and for specific industry training programs and institutions, such as the Institut national de l'image et du son and the Centre for Advanced Film Studies. The ideal is a balanced workforce with women and men sharing each occupational group. We recognize, however, that at present women are commonly found in certain positions and not in others. The education or training of women in every area is an essential prerequisite to achieving our desired workforce, and these recommendations are proactive and intended to speed the process.

33 That that there should be no less than an equal number of female and male faculty members in film/television/video educational programs. Film schools should establish links with the industry to ensure that qualified and experienced women in the industry with an interest in teaching are recruited for present and future faculty needs.

34 That all schools or institutions with film, television, or video programs including training programs specifically designed for film/television training (for example, Institut national de l'image et du son and the Centre for Advanced Film Studies) should study their personnel policies and collective agreements to identify and remove systemic discrimination in the hiring of women and that appointments of female faculty be made at a level and pay commensurate with their qualifications.

35 That all schools or institutions with film, television, or video programs establish a goal of having an equal number of female and male students admitted to film/video educational programs. That women should be recruited actively and aggressively to meet this goal, beginning in secondary school, and that all women – including aboriginal peoples, visible minorities, and the disabled – be encouraged to try non-traditional areas of study.

36 That a code of ethics should be adopted by all schools or institutions with film, television, or video programs outlining appropriate relations between faculty and students, and indicating when inappropriate relations constitute a breach of a 'relationship of trust.' The policy on sexual harassment established by the Canadian Association of University Teachers should be considered in establishing such a code of ethics.

37 That there should be no less than an equal representation of men and women on all program advisory, curriculum, student admissions, and faculty appointments committees. Women from the industry should be recruited actively and aggressively to assist.

38 That schools or institutions with film, television, and video programs document the current higher drop-out rate for women than men from film/video programs. They should cooperate in examining the possible causes and, once these are identified, they should institute structural changes to admissions policy, program of study, faculty, provision of role models as appropriate.

39 That schools and institutions with film, television, or video programs encourage more women to train in non-traditional occupations in the industry. To this end scholarships should be set up for women in non-traditional areas.

40 That schools or institutions with film, television, or video programs continue to develop links with the industry to assist students in the transition to the workforce.

41 That cooperative training programs with educational institutions be pursued that equal representation of men and women be ensured. Women should be targeted particularly for non-traditional technical jobs.

42 That the Canadian Broadcasting Corporation and the National Film Board of Canada, as public institutions, address the unequal position of women in the industry and design special programs for women to upgrade skills and to provide training in new skills.

43 That an independent watchdog organization be created to monitor progress and to communicate the need for change.

44 That the Women's Bureau of the Department of Labour should make money available to set up an education program for men in the industry to make them more aware of their actions and biases that serve to exclude or intimidate women and to understand that biological differences should not be used as the foundation for financial or social inequity.

RECOMMENDATIONS:
The Private Sector

The private sector of the film and television industry encompasses production companies, private broadcasters including all the various cable television companies, laboratories, distributors, and exhibitors.

EMPLOYMENT
We urge management of private sector companies to adopt a corporate policy that conforms with the following recommendations.

45 That management of private sector companies establish the objective of equality in all job categories, including senior management, and that achieving equality be added to performance appraisals of senior managers.

46 That management of private sector companies establish as a policy that every short list of job candidates include at least one woman.

47 That management of private sector companies find innovative means of finding women job candidates and that they recruit women agressively.

48 That management of private sector companies establish as a policy that every short list of job candidates include representation from the designated groups of visible minorities, people with disabilities, and aboriginal peoples.

49 That management of production companies examine their budgets and programs and ensure that amounts are divided equally between men and women in each program category.

50 That management of private sector companies establish apprenticeship programs for women in cooperation with the unions, associations, and guilds. These programs should target non-traditional jobs for particular attention.

51 That management of all private sector companies establish corporate policies regarding sexual harassment with appropriate reporting channels and that these policies be promoted throughout the company.

52 That private broadcasters, working in conjunction with the Canadian Association of Broadcasters, should set up professional development courses and workshops for women in management and senior creative positions.

INVESTMENT

53 That management of banks and other private lenders initiate programs for loan officers and bank managers to sensitize them to the concerns of women seeking private sector investment. Government agencies, such as Telefilm Canada or the provincial agencies, should assist women producers seeking private-sector investment.

ORGANIZATIONS AND ASSOCIATIONS

54   That industry organizations should actively participate in the process of review of the federal Employment Equity Act, 1986, to ensure that its terms reflect their concerns.

55   That industry organizations monitor the actions of the employment equity branch of Employment Canada; if it sets up a new employment equity commission with enforcement power, that industry organizations work to ensure that the rules and policies of the new commission are fair.

56   That industry organizations cooperate in setting up two committees, to monitor the CRTC's implementation of the new Broadcasting Act, in particular the broadcasting policy providing for "employment opportunities" and "equal rights."

57   That Toronto Women in Film and Television, Moitié-Moitié, and other women's industry organizations intervene in Canadian Radio-television and Telecommunications Commission licence-renewal hearings where, in the view of those organizations, broadcasters have not adhered to the approved guidelines on portrayal equity.

58   That the traditional craft unions establish the goal of increasing the numbers of women in the industry, and that this goal be monitored at the union apprentice level and the job interview level. That the goal of having no less than 50 per cent of the persons interviewed be in the target groups.

59   That industry guilds and unions provide information or courses for women to assist them in overcoming barriers to membership and employment.

60   That the Canadian Film and Television Producers Association and the Canadian Association of Broadcasters should initiate an education program for their members in cooperation with such government programs as that outlined in recommendation 44 to make men in the industry more aware of their actions and biases that serve to exclude or intimidate women and to understand that biological differences should not be used as the foundation for financial or social inequity.

MENTORING

61   That industry organizations should be consulted in the setting up of support networks for women, and for women in the other designated groups, especially in the technical areas.

62   That industry organizations such as Toronto Women in Film and Television offer student memberships to provide female students with mentors.

FURTHER STUDY

63   That federal and provincial human rights bodies be requested to carry out a study of sexual harassment in the film and television industry, its prevalence, and impact and make recommendations.

64   That industry unions, guilds, and associations investigate alternative ways of structuring working conditions for workers with family responsibilities, including looking at the way the film and television industry functions in other countries.

65   That a committee composed of representatives of the industry unions, guilds, and associations cooperate on a study to establish pay equity for the industry.

Contributors

Lisa Airst is a researcher at CBC's Disability Network. She has been a free-lance writer on political issues. Airst has a learning disability and in 1991 researched and conducted interviews for a 30-minute special on that subject.

Kay Armatage is a filmmaker, senior programmer for the Toronto Festival of Festivals, and associate professor at the University of Toronto. She has published extensively on women's cinema and feminist film theory in Canadian journals. Her films are *Jill Johnston* (1977); *Gertrude & Alice In Passing* (1978); *Bed and Sofa* (1979); *Speak Body* (1979); *Striptease* (1980); *Storytelling* (1983); *Artist on Fire: The Work of Joyce Wieland* (1987).

Pat Armstrong is chair of the sociology department of York University, Downsview, Ontario. She is co-author with Hugh Armstrong of *The Double Ghetto: Canadian Women and Their Segregated Work* (Toronto: McClelland and Stewart 1984), *A Working Majority: What Women Must Do for Pay* (Ottawa: Canadian Advisory Council on the Status of Women 1983), and *Theorizing Women's Work* (Toronto: Garamond 1990), and sole author of *Labour Pains: Women's Work in Crisis* (Toronto: Women's Press 1984).

Paula J. Caplan is professor of applied psychology at the Ontario Institute for Studies in Education and assistant professor of psychiatry and lecturer in women's studies at University of Toronto. She is author of *Between Women: Lowering the Barriers* (Toronto: Personal Library 1981), *The Myth of Women's Masochism* (New York: New American Library 1987), and *Don't Blame Mother: Mending the Mother-Daughter Relationship* (New York: Harper and Row 1989).

Susan Crean is a writer and columnist who worked as a current affairs journalist and producer in television in the 1970s. Her books include *Newsworthy: The Lives of Media Women* (Halifax: Goodread Biographies) and *In* *the Name of the Fathers: The Story Behind Child Custody* (Toronto: Second Story Press 1990). In 1989-90 she was awarded the first appointment to the Maclean-Hunter chair in creative non-fiction and business writing at the University of British Columbia.

Jocelyne Denault teaches film at the Cegep de St-Laurent. She is writing her PhD thesis in history for the Université de Montréal on the history of women in film in Quebec and is collaborating on a research program at the Université du Québec à Montréal on the problems women face in gaining access to film direction in Quebec.

Linda Silver Dranoff is a practising family lawyer, writer, and activist with a special interest in women's issues. She is author of *Every Woman's Guide to the Law* (Toronto: Fitzhenry and Whiteside 1985) and a history, *Women in Canadian Law* (Toronto: Fitzhenry and Whiteside 1977), and has written a monthly column for *Chatelaine Magazine* since 1979. She spearheaded the drive for equal sharing of family property in Ontario, and has been an advisor to the Ontario government on women's issues.

Rita Shelton Deverell is the producer of Vision TV's flagship human affairs show, "It's About Time," and network anchor. She has worked as an actor, host-interviewer for CBC's "Take 30," "Access," and "Regina Noon," and director of the Regina School of Journalism. Deverell's doctoral work was in arts policy.

Louise Lamarre studied film production at Concordia University and produced her first short documentary *Le vernissage* in 1980. For the next ten years she worked on numerous shorts, both drama and documentary, television programs, and advertising. Fascinated by history she published a book on Jacques Cartier in 1984. She is at present working on her first feature film.

Daisy Lee is an independent film procucer/director. She studied radio and television arts at Ryerson Polytechnical Institute. Lee's film, *The Morning Zoo*, reflects the participation of her Chinese-Canadian family and other families in the Ontario Food Terminal, and has been broadcast on CBC and Vision.

Linda R. Lewis is a professor and former program director for film studies in the Film and Photography Department at Ryerson Polytechnical Institute. Her subjects include film theory and history and design for film. In addition to having used film to explore issues of importance to women, her writing and curating focus on Canadian design history.

Iolande Cadrin-Rossignol has been a scriptwriter, director, and broadcaster for many years, working in both the public and the private sectors. Her film credits as author include *Rencontre avec une femme remarquable* and *Contes des mille-et-un-jours*, two studies of the role of women in Quebec society. She is currently working as scriptwriter on various productions while producing the feature film *Menaud Maître-Draveur*, for which she wrote the screen adaptation.

Armande Saint-Jean has been a journalist and broadcaster in radio and television for Radio-Canada and Radio-Québec for some 25 years. She specializes in current affairs and has directed various programs and documentaries, especially on women's issues and the women's movement. She is author of *Pour en finir avec le patriacat* (1983) and is currently professor in the communications department of Université du Québec à Montréal.

Diane Silverman is a Toronto-based freelance writer and broadcaster, working in print, television current affairs, film and radio documentary. In 1983 she won the ACTRA national radio award in the best writer/broadcaster category for her program on the death of a child, "How Shall We Live without You," and in 1989 won the same award for a radio documentary, "HMS Revenge: Aboard the Polaris."

Louise Surprenant studied cinema and television in Brussels before working as a cinematographer at the National Film Board and working on various film productions. After studying international administration at ENAP, she directed Vidéographe Inc. before returning to university to take an MA in communications. Her company Inter-Férences promotes films in Europe.

Margaret Visser teaches classics at York University and contributes programs to CBC Radio's "Morningside" and "The Arts Tonight," among others in Canada as well as the United States and Britain. A feature program on her life was produced in 1988 and has aired on CBC TV. She is a contributing editor to *Saturday Night* and her prize-winning book, *Much Depends on Dinner* (Toronto: McClelland and Stewart 1989), discusses the history and mythology of food. *The Rituals of Dinner* (Toronto: Harper Collins 1991) is on the history and mythology of table manners.

Kealy Wilkinson is a writer, broadcaster, and broadcasting consultant now living in Toronto, she has worked in both radio and television, on air and in production and management for close to 30 years. She has a special interest in licensing and regulation, service and system design.

Index